Making Needlecraft Landscapes

Making Needlecraft Landscapes

MARY CARROLL

ST. MARTIN'S PRESS
New York

ACKNOWLEDGEMENTS

I would like to thank all those involved in organising the initial competition, the generous craftswomen who entered the competition and gave their work freely for a good cause, and the companies who kindly donated prizes for the winners.

Very special thanks on my part to Christine Baddeley and Sue Whiting, who were an invaluable help in compiling the instructions for all thirty-two designs.

Thank-you also to Clare & Newman Design Associates Ltd for clear and concise drawings, and to John Cook for his very professional photography.

Last but not least, thanks to Orlando Murrin for his help and advice in compiling the complete work.

(*frontispiece*) Welsh Bay, see page 116

ISBN 0-312-50735-6
ISBN 0-312-50734-8 (pbk.)

Text and illustrations © David & Charles,
 Living Magazine and
 the British Needlecrafts
 Council 1986

Phototypeset by Typesetters (Birmingham) Ltd, Smethwick, West Midlands and printed in The Netherlands by Smeets Offset BV, Weert

Published in Great Britain in 1986 by David & Charles Publishers

Contents

The Old Mill see page 104

Introduction

Cancer has become part of today's world – whether we read about it in the newspapers or magazines, know a friend or relative who has had it, or even closer to home, have been involved with it ourselves. It is certainly one of today's ironies that despite all the advances made in technology, from landing on the moon to giving an individual a new heart, we are still desperately trying to find a cure for the killer disease.

Part of the problem with cancer is that the longer it is left without treatment, the more dramatic is the decline – so catching it in the bud is very important; in very many instances it can be removed, resulting in a clean bill of health.

It was with this in mind that *Living Magazine* launched a campaign to help the Women's National Cancer Control Campaign (WNCCC) make women more aware of cervical and breast cancer and the importance of regular screening. The money raised would go towards providing mobile units which would be sent all over Great Britain to give women an accessible screening facility, together with any assistance or advice they might need.

To help raise funds, *Living Magazine* got together with the British Needlecrafts Council and the tourist boards of England, Wales, Scotland and Northern Ireland and devised a competition involving creative embroidery. The brief was to 'design a picture of Britain using any type of work from tapestry or weaving to knitting or embroidery, the only proviso being that a needle should be used at some stage of the design.'

From the many hundreds of entries, all of which were worked to a very high standard, thirty-two were chosen – and the result is this book.

As you look through the many wonderful designs you will realise just how individual the ideas are, some worked from holiday snapshots, others from a lingering memory. The different stitches and techniques have been used in ever-surprising ways. Fabrics have been chosen with great care and thought so that the result reflects the scene depicted.

It is this individuality that makes each piece unique. To make it possible for you to capture beautiful Britain, we have given instructions for each picture, together with all the background information you might need. To re-create each stitch and line of work would be impossible, so we have given a basic guide from which you can create your own individual piece, worked in your own particular way. The craftswomen concerned have very generously donated their work to an auction in aid of the campaign and, together with the royalties from this book, we hope it will further the search for a cure and increase screening facilities for breast and cervical cancer.

Thank-you to everyone who entered the competition; I hope that like me you will be inspired by the wonderful ideas created by British craftswomen and take up your needle to re-create some scene from beautiful Britain.

Mary Carroll
Living Magazine

1
The Design

The subject and how it is interpreted are all-important in making a piece of embroidery successful. There are many different sources of inspiration, all of which will give you a different feeling for what you are looking to create.

Many of the designs in this book have been taken from lasting memories of happy day-outings or longer holidays. Postcards and holiday snapshots have been used as references for proportion and colour. Be sure to pick a subject in which you are interested, so that the enthusiasm for working the piece is kept up until it is finished. It does also help if the subject has a focal point which leads the eye around the work.

If you find the idea of a full landscape rather daunting, start on a small piece of work. The smallest subject – a leaf, a stone – will, if looked at closely, develop into a complex mix of colour and texture that can be interpreted in a multitude of interesting ways using textural embroidery and other techniques. Look at your chosen subject carefully: what might appear as a patch of green grass is really a mass of varying shades, ranging from dark to light green, from yellow to ochre – all colours that could be translated into stitches using colourful threads.

The Cottage of Gaddesby by Jane Grewcock is a wonderful example of perception. She has used a wealth of shades to depict the smallest of bushes. Darker shades are used for areas where the bush is in shadow, with lighter shades as it faces the light. The bush takes on a truly three-dimensional feel: it looks so real you could almost touch it.

An alternative to choosing a complete scene as your inspiration could be taking a section of a picture or a postcard. Kate Thorp's Summer

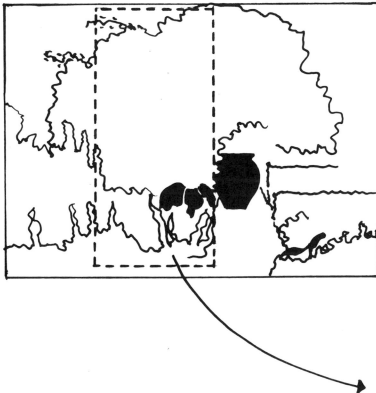

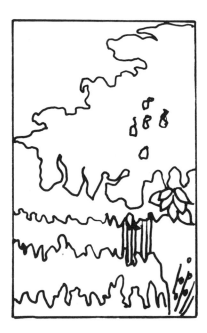

Fig 1 A small area of a picture postcard was used as inspiration by Kate Thorp in Summer Memories

Memories demonstrates this beautifully. As inspiration for her design she took a small section of a picture postcard, enlarged the idea, then worked it in interesting stitches and yarns into a beautiful three-dimensional picture. Small studies such as this can be very good for the beginner – the work can be controlled, it will take comparatively less time to do and the use of colour, texture and tone can be tried over a small area.

If you are interested in appliqué techniques, the fabrics you choose can often be a good source of inspiration. Isabel Blincow's appliqué designs are stunning examples of good choice of fabric. She has picked both furnishing and dress fabrics that reflect the look of a hillside or the roof of a cottage. It is this attention to detail that makes her pieces so well executed and such a pleasure to look at.

Draw your design on paper first. The drawing doesn't have to reflect every detail, just the main design lines. Try applying colour with crayons to give a feeling of colour and depth. This colour can be developed in the stitchery you use or in the application of fabrics. Use books, posters, maps or photographs to get the proportions right and don't be afraid to follow the shape and design they show. You should find that the more you study the sections of your design and how it really appears, the more lifelike your work will become.

Do try out stitch techniques before you start on the piece of work. You will probably have some idea as to whether you are going to use hand or machine embroidery, whether you are going to introduce fabrics, or whether you even plan to make and dye the yarn to be used within the design.

The technique you use will determine the backing fabric most suitable for your design (see Chapter 3). Preparing all the knowledge and equipment for your piece will make the working of the design far more enjoyable and you will see for yourself how a simple plan can develop into an interesting use of ideas and techniques that is very much in your handwriting.

Transferring your design onto fabric

Each design in this book is provided with a line drawing so that the correct scale and detail of the work can be interpreted. Although a little time-consuming, it is a good idea to transfer the design onto fabric before the fabric is stretched in a frame ready for working.

Following the centimetre measurements given on each diagram, draw a size-grid on tracing paper, then, following the lines given, draw in the design details.

The design should next be reproduced on the base fabric using one of a variety of different methods. You'll probably find, or have already, a

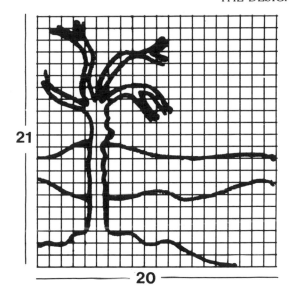

Fig 2 Draw a grid to the size of the design required, marking in the design lines

system of transferring your design that works best for you.

A popular method suitable for simple designs uses dressmaker's carbon. This paper, unlike regular office carbon, does not smudge and is placed between the tracing paper and the fabric with all the layers taped down to prevent movement. Simply trace over the lines with a sharp, hard pencil.

Another common method, suitable for more intricate designs, is the 'prick and pounce' method. Using a crewel needle, small holes are made along each of the design lines drawn out on tracing paper. The pricked paper is then placed over the base fabric and stuck firmly down to a board. Talcum powder is pressed through the prick holes using a small pad of rolled cloth or cotton wool to work it in. Remove the tracing paper and while the dots are still intact, join up the lines using a washable embroidery pencil. If you are working on a white base fabric, a small amount of powdered charcoal can be added to the talcum powder so that the dots will be defined on the base fabric.

Transfer pencils, sold in most embroidery departments, can be useful, although they are only advisable for very simple designs. The lines on the tracing paper are traced over using the transfer pencil. The tracing is then placed face down on the base fabric and 'set' to the fabric using a hot iron. It is worth remembering, however, that if you use this method the design will appear in reverse on the base fabric.

Depending on the fabric used, the old method of window tracing can always be relied on. Simply tape the tracing paper and then the base fabric to a well-lit window, and lightly pencil over the lines.

2
Materials and Tools

Backing Fabric

The backing fabric forms the base for the design and as you will see from the ideas included in this book, often indicates which threads and colours are used. It is important to choose the right fabric for the design and technique you have decided on, but as a general rule, use a closely woven even-weave fabric – linen, cotton and rayon are good fabrics to use as bases.

If you are a beginner, counted-thread fabric, which is available in needlecraft departments, will give a good result. The warp and weft threads can be counted easily and give a guide for the stitches to be worked over. You don't, however, have to spend money on your base material if you have any oddments of furnishing or dress fabric; even sheeting makes a good base. But do bear in mind that the look and texture of the fabric adds considerably to the design and can often inspire the original idea.

Take note also of the fabric's fibre content. This is important if you are thinking of combining fabric painting and embroidery in one piece. Paints need to be 'fixed' to the fabric with a hot iron, so a natural fibre such as cotton is most suitable. You may, as several women have done, base your design on the colour of the fabric. Gillian Hickman's Tranquillity illustrates this idea well: the soft-green fabric forms the base of the design, and colour and texture are added in stitchery.

Or you may like to use a less conventional fabric. Isabel Blincow has done this in her English Cornfield. She has used roller-blind fabric, applied misty shades of coloured car spray paints then introduced a three-dimensional quality to the design with machine embroidery.

Another idea is to start with a sheer fabric and weave yarn and fabric strips through this in a more abstract design. Whichever fabric you choose, make sure that the piece of cloth is of an adequate size; you'll need plenty of space around the design area to attach the fabric to your working frame.

Interlinings

These can be bonded fabrics such as Vilene – both iron-on and sew-in are suitable – or woven fabrics such as mull, calico or canvas. They are attached to the wrong side of the piece to give it 'body' as it is being worked or to help keep it in shape when it has been completed.

You may find it especially helpful when working machine embroidery to attach interlining to the base fabric before you set it in a frame. This helps to form a firm base that will not distort under the machine, especially if the base fabric is fine or loosely woven.

A piece of work removed from a frame after it is completed can sometimes, however carefully worked, be slightly distorted. This can be rectified by pinning the shape out to the original square or rectangle and applying a fine layer of fusible interlining to the wrong side.

Threads

Stranded cotton is perhaps the most popular choice of thread for beginners and experienced needlewomen alike. Made by several leading companies, it is available in a wide range of colours including shaded colours that change from dark to light tones throughout one skein. It is a versatile thread which easily divides into six single strands. These can be used in various numbers to create different stitch thicknesses.

Soft embroidery threads are slightly thicker than stranded cotton and are not generally split. Their soft feel gives stitches a rich smooth texture and possibly more subtlety of colour than stranded cotton.

Coton à broder is about as thick as embroidery thread and very often highly twisted. You will probably find, however, that the colour range is not quite as extensive as for the other threads.

Tapestry wool is another popular yarn used extensively for canvas work and has a softer, warmer feel and look than cotton thread. The wool is refined to give a good, even texture of thread for stitchery and the colours of this natural yarn can be extremely subtle.

Knitting and crochet yarns can also be used if a more fancy thread is required and look particularly effective couched to the surface of the base fabric. The range these days is wide and varied, with

Sandy Shore, which uses an interesting array of oddments, see
page 64

cotton, wool and mohair yarns providing a wealth of texture and colour.

If you are working to a budget, old sweaters unravelled will give a good source of yarn; alternatively, fabric cut into narrow strips can provide an original thread easily woven into canvas.

Glitter threads are now more widely available and can be used to highlight areas of your design – a reflection, the sunshine on a roof or rays of light on rigging. Some of the finer qualities can be wound onto the bobbin of your machine for intricate machine work and the thicker ones look good couched to the design areas.

Needles

A good needle is essential, whether you are to embroider by machine or hand. The wrong needle will make the work seem tedious and produce poor-quality stitches.

Sharps needles have a fine eye and should be of medium length. They are suitable for use with fine cotton threads and one or two strands of stranded cotton.

Crewel needles are long and sharp, with a larger eye which is able to take the six strands of stranded cotton and coton à broder. Size 5 needles have a slightly larger eye than size 6–8 crewel needles, and are able to take tapestry wool.

Tapestry needles have a blunt end and are most generally used for canvas work, where holes do not need to be made by the needle.

Beading needles are particularly fine so that the whole length of the needle including the eye will fit through the eye of the bead.

Leather needles have a three-cornered point to allow the needle to pierce the leather or suede as it is sewn.

Frames

No less important than the right needle is the correct frame. For the beginner and most experienced worker alike, the frame provides a stretched area to work on, at the same time giving a

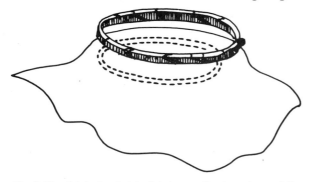

Fig 3 The fabric is stretched between the two rings of the tambour frame

professional finish to the piece being worked. From the smallest design to the largest format, it is always possible to tell a piece worked on a frame.

Using a frame does mean you have to make an initial outlay, so if you are experimenting with ideas, start with an inexpensive tambour frame. The tambour frame consists of two rings which fit together, with the outside ring having a tightening screw. Some can be obtained with a clamp attached for use on a table, others can simply be held in the hand and for this reason can be easily transported from place to place. The base fabric is placed between the two rings with the screw tightened, giving the fabric the appearance of a drum top. It is a good idea to wrap a strip of fine fabric around the entire inner circle, firstly to protect the base fabric and secondly to help the fabric grip the ring. Because the fabric is very tightly stretched, keeping it fixed in the frame over a period of months may distort it; so remove the work at regular intervals to let the fabric relax.

The rectangular frame is slightly more advanced than the tambour, though not significantly more efficient. The frame can be held on your lap as you work or set on a floor-standing attachment – a variety of different sizes is available.

The frame consists of a top and bottom roller between which the top and bottom edges of the base fabric are stretched. The sides of the base fabric are held taut by tension threads which can be altered according to how tight you want the work to be. A good border should be left around the design area so that the work can be attached to the frame without encroaching on the design.

This type of frame is particularly good for canvas work and if you plan to make this form of embroidery a hobby it is worthwhile investing in a good quality frame. An alternative to this rather expensive outlay is a frame made out of stretcher bars available from artists' shops. Two bars should be bought to form the sides of the frame and two for the top and bottom. They are available in various sizes, allowing you to make up a frame to the size you require. You simply construct the frame then stretch the work over the shape and fix to the frame with tacks or drawing pins.

Simple hand-made frames or old picture frames can make adequate pieces of equipment and many a beautiful piece of work has been executed on one of these. The base fabric is held in place around the wooden edges by drawing pins or staples. Make sure, though, that as you secure the fabric in position, the threads of the fabric are at right-angles to the framework.

Sewing Machine

Obviously the sewing machine is essential for machine embroidery, although a mass of attach-

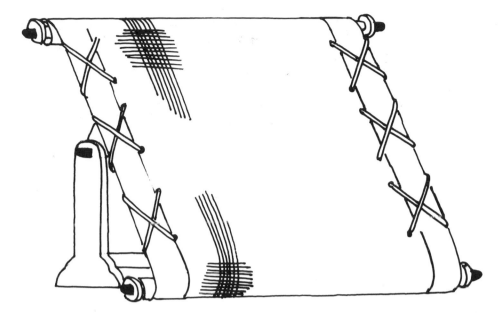

Fig 4 The rectangular frame is suitable for all embroidery, especially canvas work

ments and fancy stitches are not necessary. Beautiful pieces can be produced with just straight and zigzag stitch and with the presser foot removed, creative random effects can be obtained by moving the work around under the needle. As in hand sewing, it is important to have the right thickness of needle for the fabric being worked and a new needle at the start of a piece of work is always a good move.

Scissors and Pins

A good selection of scissors is important if you are going to take up embroidery as a hobby. They are expensive, so build up a collection as you progress. For beginners, a pair of small embroidery scissors with sharp points is useful for cutting off threads and a larger pair of sharp dressmaker's scissors will be helpful for cutting fabric. Good pins are also important. Old pins can, if left in the base fabric, leave small marks which will be difficult to remove. Wedding-dress pins are particularly good, being very long and fine, or alternatively, the finest dressmaking pins you can find.

Fabric Paints

The use of fabric paints with embroidery is a technique becoming increasingly popular among designers in every area of embroidery work. The paints are becoming more widely available, with Dylon Color Fun stocked in most large department stores and art shops (an alternative stockist is given in Stockists). They are simply painted onto the fabric with an artist's brush, then ironed on the wrong side of the work to set the design. They can also be watered down slightly and then placed in an airbrush. Sprayed onto the fabric, the paint will give a misty, speckled effect which is most attractive as a base for textured stitchery.

Glue

Glue is useful if pieces of fabric or thread need to be attached to the surface of the base fabric and stitching is not appropriate. Always use a glue that dries clear such as Copydex or UHU and use very sparingly to prevent the glue showing on the right side.

Spray glue, such as that made by 3M, is particularly useful if large areas of fabric are to be stuck down to the base fabric. Do remember, however, that this type of glue should be used in a well-ventilated room and areas around the design should be covered with newspaper to avoid the glue settling on other surfaces.

Unusual Design Elements

The texture of embroidery work can be greatly enhanced by all sorts of oddments you may have in your sewing box or around the home. The design Sandy Shore is a perfect example of this, with every conceivable oddment being used to depict the scene and all the details in it.

This technique applies particularly to appliqué, where unusual fabrics and oddments can be applied to the design, giving the work originality and depth. Cord, lace, ribbon, beads, sequins, braids and mesh are just a few of the possible oddments that might bring interest and individuality to your piece.

Cottage of Gaddesby, showing a wonderful use of basic straight stitch, see page 40

3
Techniques and Stitches

This chapter is to help you decide which technique you would like to use for your design, be it by hand or machine; or perhaps you might like to follow the example of many of the craftswomen whose work is illustrated here, by cleverly combining several design techniques in one piece of work.

Hand Embroidery

A simple piece of fabric can be turned into a beautiful and rewarding design with just a needle and thread. Each of the designs in the book displays an inventive use of the stitch, from the simplest running stitch to the more complicated embroidery techniques.

The sewing machine of today, with all its gadgets and stitches, has created another type of embroidery again, with the work obviously being completed at greater speed. However, although the machine has many advantages which should be considered, many women still prefer the creativity hand embroidery allows; each stitch can be worked differently from the next, and the therapeutic value of hand stitching can be tremendous.

Hand embroidery depends greatly on the sympathetic use of fabric, thread, stitch and colour. It is a good idea to try out various stitches in different coloured threads and on different base fabrics to see how they work with each other. Striking effects can be produced with shiny yarns used simply on a matt background or with thick threads and yarns on a tweedy fabric.

Trying out stitches will give you an idea of the cover a stitch gives. You may like to work stitches packed tightly together, or let the base fabric show through in areas to give the design a feeling of space.

Experiment with the size of the stitches. A variety of different-sized stitches can be worked closely together, giving a graduated feel to the work. This works especially well with satin stitch. Worked at different lengths and angles, this stitch will create various tones of thread just through the play of light on the work. Stitches can be worked over each other to produce a very dense piece of work or to create an illusion of depth.

The best way of using the stitches will become more apparent as you work with them. The selection of stitches given below includes all those used in the designs, together with a few extras you may also like to try. They have been divided into categories: stitches that are suitable for outline stitchery; filling stitches suitable for covering an area of work; and textural stitches that will create a three-dimensional effect. As you can see from the designs, though, none of the guidelines has to be stuck to rigidly. Play around with the ideas as much as you like – they can always be undone quickly and tried again.

Please note that the diagrams shown can be worked by a right-handed person. If you are left-handed, place the diagram in front of a mirror and follow the diagram in the mirror image.

Outlining Stitches

These are suitable for defining an edge or shape in the design. Several of the stitches may seem too simple for creating elaborate embroidery, but used in the right way, they can create imaginative effects. The Cottage of Gaddesby by Jane Grewcock shows a wonderful use of the most basic stitch, the straight or running stitch.

Straight Stitch

With the needle brought through to the right side of the fabric, work stitches evenly along a straight line; keep the stitches the same length on the wrong and right sides of the fabric.

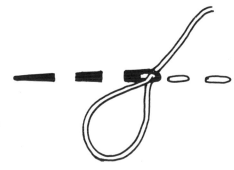

Fig 5 Straight stitch

Back Stitch

This is a basic stitch, giving a slightly more raised effect than straight stitch. Bring the needle out from the back of the fabric, and take a small stitch backwards. Bring the needle out again, a stitch-length in front of the first stitch, and take another stitch backwards. A small gap can be left in between each stitch if a dotted-line effect is required.

Blanket Stitch

A strong, angular stitch, blanket stitch is often used in hand-appliqué work for neatening a fabric edge and applying it to the base fabric at the same time. It is usually worked evenly spaced out, but worked close together it can form a buttonhole stitch.

Work the stitch from left to right, imagining that you have a top and bottom line separated by the depth which you would like the stitch to be. Bring the needle out on the lower line and make a stitch downwards, bringing the needle over the working thread. Continue in this way, keeping the bottom sections of the stitch in line.

Cable Stitch

A very regular outline stitch, cable stitch can also be used as a satisfactory filling stitch. It is basically a back-stitch formation. Working from left to right, make one stitch to the right with the working thread above the needle. Bring the needle through to the right side of the fabric, halfway along the stitch just worked (with the working thread below the needle). Work another stitch with the thread above the needle, coming out on the right side at the end of the previous stitch.

Chain Stitch

This is a decorative stitch which is particularly good for outlining areas of the design. The worked stitch forms loops on the right side, with a back stitch on the wrong side.

Bring the needle through onto the right side of the design line and holding the working thread above or below the line with the left thumb, insert the needle at the place where it first emerged. Bring the needle out a little further along the design line and pull the needle through, keeping the loop of working thread under the needle point.

Detached chain stitch is worked in the same way, the only difference being that each stitch is separate. When the loop of thread has been formed, take a small stitch over the top of the loop to hold it down, leave a space and bring the needle out where the base of the next stitch is to be worked.

Knotted Chain Stitch

This is a fancy development of the chain stitch, and is worked from right to left. Bring the needle out to the right side of the fabric and take a small

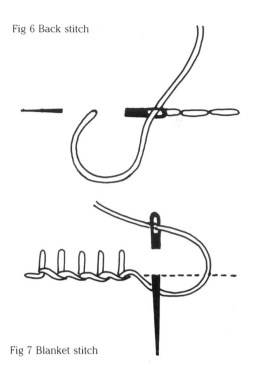

Fig 6 Back stitch

Fig 7 Blanket stitch

Fig 8 Cable stitch

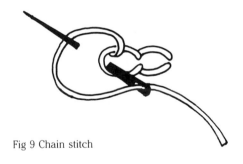

Fig 9 Chain stitch

Fig 9a Detached chain stitch

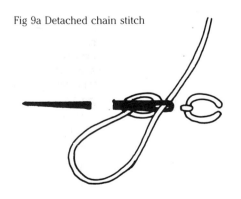

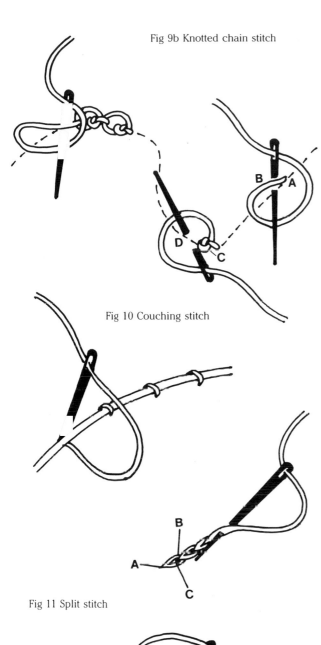

Fig 9b Knotted chain stitch

Fig 10 Couching stitch

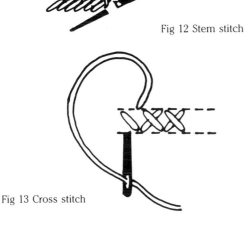

Fig 11 Split stitch

Fig 12 Stem stitch

Fig 13 Cross stitch

stitch a little distance away (A), inserting the needle at the back of the thread. Bring the needle through with the thread underneath the needle. Pass the needle back through the stitch just made (B), without piercing the fabric. Take a small stitch (C) close to the knot formed, with the thread under the needle (D).

Couching Stitch

Couching is a securing stitch which can be used to give greater depth and texture to your design. Yarn and threads which may be too thick to work in and out of the base fabric can be held down to the surface of the work using couching stitch.

Lay the thread in position on the right side of the work, taking the ends through to the wrong side (if the thread is very thick help it through with a knitting needle or crochet hook). Use a finer thread in either a matching or contrasting shade and work small stitches over the thicker thread.

Split Stitch

This stitch looks very similar to chain stitch and can be used for outlining or filling a shape. The stitch can be lengthened and shortened along the line to give a varied effect.

Bring the needle out at A and make a stitch the length of A to B. Bring the needle out at C (halfway along the stitch just formed) and through the working thread, splitting it in half. Repeat the stitch in this way from this position.

Stem Stitch

Perhaps the most common outlining stitch, stem stitch is worked from left to right.

Make a slanted stitch along the design line, then bring the needle back through the fabric halfway along the previous stitch on the lower side.

Filling Stitches

These stitches can be used to fill areas of your design with stitchery. Whole areas of sky or land can be filled using one simple stitch, or the stitch can be confined to a smaller area such as flower petals.

Cross Stitch

A beautifully simple stitch, cross stitch can be extremely effective when used as the one and only stitch worked over an entire design. A Cornish Medley, worked by Sarah Dodds, is a fine example of this with the letters of the alphabet, flowers and intricate border patterns all worked in cross stitch.

Use a good canvas or even-weave fabric for your base so that the threads can be counted to give accurate stitching.

Having decided how many threads each cross stitch is going to be worked over, bring the needle

A Cornish Medley showing clever use of the most basic cross stitch, see page 71

out at the top left-hand corner of the work. Take a diagonal stitch to the bottom right-hand corner over a counted number of threads. Bring the needle out at the bottom left-hand corner, level with where the thread emerged. Take the thread up to the top right-hand corner, through to the back and out to the front at the top left-hand corner of the next stitch to be worked.

Flat Stitch
This is particularly effective when used on petals, as it gives the shape a lovely padded texture.

Small stitches are worked alternately down each side of the shape, with the needle emerging on the right side of the cloth at the outside-line position. You may find it easier when first working this stitch to pencil in the inner and outer guidelines.

Long-and-short Stitch
This is a similar stitch to flat stitch and again works well on flower-petal shapes.

Starting at the outside edge of the shape to be worked, work a row of border stitches, using a short stitch and a long stitch alternately. On the next row, work stitches of equal length, fitting them into the spaces left by the previous row. Each subsequent row is worked with stitches of the same length.

Roumanian Stitch
This could be described as a fancy satin stitch (see below) and can look beautiful worked in a fine strand of thread, which produces the most delicate surface.

Working from left to right, take a stitch across the area to be filled, bringing the needle back to the centre of the area, keeping the thread below the needle. Take a small stitch over the thread lying flat and bring the needle out at the left-hand side of the area. Continue working the stitch in this way, making sure that the stitches are packed closely together to give a good coverage of the fabric.

Satin Stitch
This is a useful stitch, especially if large areas need to be filled. Straight stitches are worked side by side and closely together to give a 'satin' feel. Added depth can be created by using this stitch in a shaded thread. Random small blocks of satin stitch can be used to give a lighter feel to the work.

Seed Stitch
This is a small, delicate filling stitch giving a dappled embroidered effect. It consists of a small straight stitch worked singly and can be stitched at any angle.

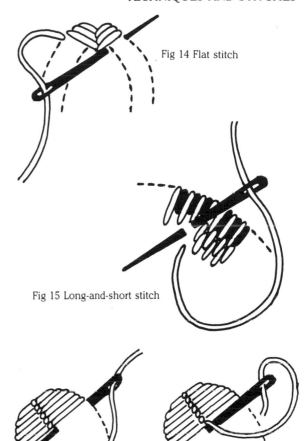

Fig 14 Flat stitch

Fig 15 Long-and-short stitch

Fig 16 Roumanian stitch

Fig 17 Satin stitch

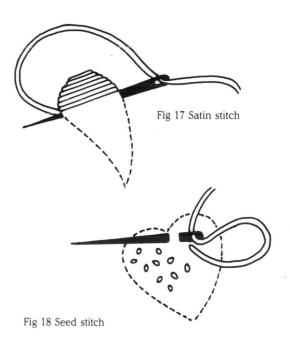

Fig 18 Seed stitch

Texture Stitches

These stitches can be used to add focal points to your design; most of them having a somewhat raised effect. They can be used in small areas or, for a heavily textured effect, worked together in a variety of thick and thin threads.

Bullion Stitch

This is a fancy, three-dimensional stitch, often used to represent flower-heads and foliage. It could be described as a long version of the French knot and is worked in a similar way.

With the needle threaded, take a back stitch the length of the stitch required and before pulling the needle right through the fabric, wind the thread several times round the needle. Hold the coiled thread on the needle with your left thumb, then take the needle point back to the beginning of the back stitch and through to the wrong side of the fabric until the stitch lies flat.

Fly Stitch

As its name suggests, this stitch resembles a fly and can be used as a decorative stitch worked in rows forming a border or singly to represent flower-heads or distant birds.

Work the stitch from left to right; bring the needle through on the left-hand side and take a stitch level and to the right of where the thread emerges (hold the working thread down with the left thumb at the same time). Bring the needle out below and halfway between these two points, catching the thread under the needle. Take a small stitch to hold the thread in place. Start again with a stitch taken to the left for a continuous row of fly stitches.

French Knot

This is a very popular and attractive textural stitch. Kate Thorp has used it beautifully in Summer Memories to depict dense flower-heads in bloom.

Bring the needle through to the right side of the fabric, then taking working thread, wind it round the needle several times. Holding the coiled thread securely on the needle with your left hand, place the needle through the fabric close to where it emerged – the knot will slip off the needle and lie in position on the fabric. Bring the needle through to the right side, in position for the next stitch.

It is a good idea to use a needle with a slender eye when working this stitch, so that the needle passes easily through the coiled thread.

Open Cretan Stitch

This decorative stitch must be worked evenly and accurately to be shown at its best. The stitches can be brought closer together to act as a filling stitch for larger areas of a design. Bring the needle out at

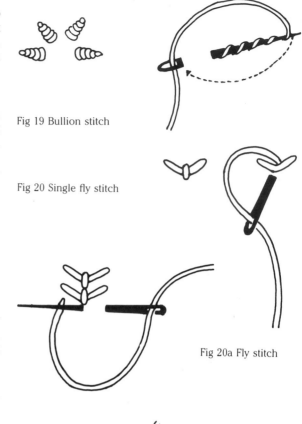

Fig 19 Bullion stitch

Fig 20 Single fly stitch

Fig 20a Fly stitch

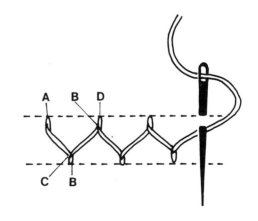

Fig 21 French knot

Fig 22 Open Cretan stitch

A. Holding the thread upwards, insert the needle on the lower imaginary line. Bring the needle out at C with the line of thread A to B held in position. Insert the needle on the top line at D and bring the needle out at E with the thread under the needle.

Pekinese Stitch

An intricate formation, Pekinese stitch has a somewhat oriental look; it consists of a row of back stitch with loops of thread worked above, below and through this base row. The stitch can be worked using just one thread for both stages or a second more elaborate thread such as glitter thread could be used for the loops.

Work a row of back stitch (see page 16). Starting with the needle brought out at the bottom left-hand corner, pass the needle under the second back stitch and back through the first back stitch (forming a top loop). With the needle at the bottom of the work, pass the needle under the third back stitch and back through the second. Repeat this formation of loops, making sure that the loops are not pulled too tightly.

Sheaf Stitch

This is a pretty stitch based on satin stitch. Groups of satin stitches of equal length are worked, and the needle is then brought through to the right side, first centrally then to the side of the group of satin stitches. Work a few overcast stitches over the middle of the threads, then take the thread back to the wrong side through the middle, where the thread first emerged.

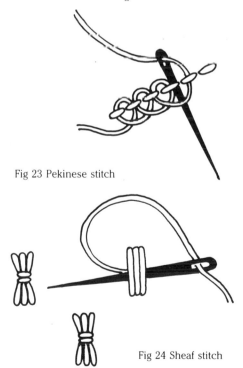

Fig 23 Pekinese stitch

Fig 24 Sheaf stitch

Machine Embroidery

Machine embroidery has become increasingly popular since the invention of the sewing machine, with the resulting designs often worked to high standard of great creativity. An embroidery worked in this technique, apart from taking comparatively less time than a hand-worked piece, has the regular and professional finish associated with a machine. There are many exciting ways of using the machine and the simplest of operations, the straight stitch, provides a wealth of ideas and textures. There are three levels of machine available for embroidery. The most basic of these is the straight-stitch machine, which produces lines of stitching which can be worked parallel to each other, perhaps using a variety of different threads or curved lines to make a shape or design. A little more sophisticated is the zigzag-stitch machine, on which the stitch width can be altered as much as the stitch length. More advanced still is the fully automated machine with a variety of set stitches available, providing a wonderful basis for unending ideas and techniques.

Whether you have a basic or fully automated machine, the embroidery can be worked in a regular way with the presser foot attached. Alternatively, this can be removed, the 'feed' of the machine lowered and the work carried out freehand by moving the fabric around at random under the machine needle.

There are many approaches open to you, but there are several hard-and-fast rules for producing a well-executed piece of machine embroidery. Firstly, the base fabric must be held tautly in position under the needle. The tambour frame is the most suitable equipment for this. The base fabric is stretched in the frame, with the inner ring wrapped in fine fabric to help protect the work; unlike hand embroidery, the work is placed under the needle with the frame facing uppermost. Remember to avoid shiny base fabrics which can appear messy and wrinkled when worked with machine embroidery.

A size 14 needle is perhaps the most suitable size; finer needles have a tendency to snap if the top and bottom threads are unbalanced or if a thick thread is being used.

Regular machine threads Nos 40 and 50 are suitable for machine embroidery, as are thicker threads such as coton à broder or stranded cotton; the thicker threads are wound onto the bobbin spool by hand with an ordinary machine thread used for the top thread. Metallic thread should be wound onto the bobbin spool in the same way, as it has a tendency to snap when used as the top thread. It is worthwhile remembering, though, that the fancy thread will be on the underside of the work, so the base fabric should be set in the frame so that the right side of the work is facing down.

The base fabric should be marked out with the design before the fabric is placed in the frame. A soft, light-coloured crayon can be used to mark out the design on the right side or alternatively a tracing of the design can be tacked to the wrong side of the work and guidelines machined through both the paper and fabric. Tear the paper away, turn the work round so the right side is facing you and work the main embroidery using these guidelines as references.

Presser-foot Machine Work

This type of machine work is controlled with the presser foot in position. This doesn't mean, however, that the resulting effects will be dull and uninteresting. Before beginning the actual design, practise on some spare base fabric. Experiment by altering the length and width of the various stitches to see what effect this has on different threads. Try altering the top and bottom tension on the machine. The top tension thread can be tightened or loosened as can the bobbin tension. Check with your instruction book as each make of machine differs slightly from the next. Couching fancy threads to the surface of the base fabric can be carried out with rows of machine embroidery. Set your machine to a fairly open work stitch such as a zigzag and holding a length of fancy thread in position on the work, machine a line of stitching over the thread to hold it down. Ribbon and braid can also be couched onto the base fabric in a similar way.

Free-Machine Embroidery

The greatest variety of techniques will undoubtedly come from using a swing-needle machine and free-machine embroidery. The design can be

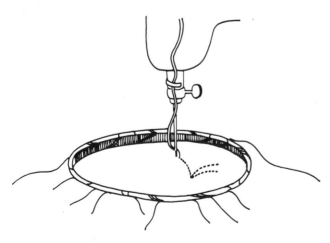

Fig 25 Free-machine embroidery with the fabric stretched in a tambour frame and the presser foot removed

developed as you work the stitch length and width and can be made to look different every few stitches.

To prepare the machine for this work, the presser foot should be removed. The 'feed' teeth on the base plate should then be lowered. (Your instruction book should explain how to do this, perhaps under the 'darning' section.) If your machine does not have this facility, a special plate can be obtained to cover the teeth for free-machine embroidery.

Thread the top and bottom threads in the normal way, making sure that both their tensions are somewhat loose. If one of the threads snaps this will be because the tension is not slack enough. While you are practising this technique use a different coloured thread in the bobbin to that used on the top so that you can see easily what is happening to the stitch and what effect altering the tension has on the right side of the work. If this is the first time you have tried this technique it is advisable to attach a darning foot to the machine. Until you are used to the way in which the needle darts around the work, this will protect your fingers as will another safety precaution, a finger shield – not expensive and worth it when you are just starting.

Place the base fabric stretched in its frame underneath the needle, right side uppermost. Holding onto the top thread and turning the wheel by hand, bring the bobbin thread up onto the top of the base fabric. Holding both threads on the top of the work, turn the wheel by hand until the needle goes down into the hole through which the bottom thread has come. Lower the presser-foot lever (although the presser foot is no longer attached, this lever affects the top tension) and still holding the two threads on the top, start machining. Once the work has been started the two threads can be cut off close to the work. Run the machine at a medium pace, moving the frame slowly around to give a fluid feel to the stitches. To move from one area of the work to another, raise the needle and the presser foot, replace the needle over the area to be worked, lower the needle into the work, then lower the presser foot and continue stitching.

As you became more experienced and controlled at working the machine, you can practise altering the top and bottom tensions. Loosening the bottom tension considerably gives a loose, crunchy feel to the right side of the work. Try out both straight and zigzag stitch, altering the stitch size for a different effect again. Do, however, alter

English Cornfield, a free-machine embroidered scene, see page 52

the tension in small stages so that you can determine exactly what your machine can do; you will probably find these small changes more interesting than dramatic ones.

As you become more familiar with this technique, you will find that you will produce the best work with your elbows down, the thumb and little finger of each hand lying against the frame, and the remaining fingers lying just inside the frame area. Always take great care when removing the work from the machine, especially if the needle is unguarded.

Quilting

Quilting is stitching worked either by hand or machine through layers of fabric and wadding to give a raised textural effect. For many years, even centuries, it has been used as an art form in the shape of bed quilts, which use stitch-patterns steeped in history. Many of the women in this book have, however, used quilting in a more abstract way, applying the art to a particular area of the work to depict a textural scene. Janet Phillips's Rain Clouds Over The Beacons shows how quilting and fabric painting can be used to reflect stormy clouds of great depth and reality.

Whether it is to be worked by hand or machine, the quilting consists of three layers – the backing or base fabric, a wadding layer and a top layer. The backing fabric may well be the base fabric you have chosen or alternatively, if the complete area of design is to be worked in quilting, any oddment of fabric or sheeting can be used for this purpose. The wadding can be terylene or cotton, depending on the look you want to create. Terylene wadding comes in a variety of weights which denote the thickness and is generally softer than cotton wadding. The top layer can be whatever material you have chosen for your design. Shiny and pile fabrics give particularly interesting effects when quilted.

All three layers should be tacked together around the outside edges and with several rows of tacking worked over the entire quilting area, at regular intervals and parallel or at right angles to the straight grain of the fabric. This initial preparation will make the stitching process much easier and far more successful.

Hand quilting should be sewn using a needle threaded with strong sewing thread and a small running or back stitch worked along the lines of the design. Take care not to pull the stitches too tightly as this will give a messy finished effect. Several of the designers in this book have preferred to use a single stitch at random over the quilting area, giving a particularly padded effect.

Machine quilting gives slightly harder lines than hand quilting and lends itself to more modern pieces of work. The machine should be set to a straight stitch of average length and the presser-foot tension released a little so that the three layers pass easily through the machine. You may find that fixing the work to a frame will help to keep the piece straight and all the layers together. Other experiments can be tried using more fancy machine stitches, which give a slightly more compact feel to the work.

Appliqué

Appliqué is the application of one fabric to another and like quilting can be worked using a hand or machine technique.

The appliqué fabrics are secured to the base fabric which can be chosen from a variety of different materials – strong cotton, calico, furnishing and dress fabrics all being suitable, depending on whether the base fabric is going to show in the completed piece of work. Pick your appliqué fabric carefully. It should be equal to or even lighter in weight than the base fabric; if several different fabrics are to be used, they should complement each other in colour and texture when grouped together. Isabel Blincow's designs are shining examples of care, thought and flair put into the choice of fabrics. It is an added plus if the fabrics don't fray easily but if you find a fraying fabric you definitely want to use, iron a lightweight fusible interlining to the wrong side of the fabric to give it 'body' and stability.

Cutting out the Appliqué Shapes

Either following one of the designs given or, if designing your own, draw the work to full size on a piece of tracing or plain paper. Trace off each separate piece of the appliqué, noting which fabric it will be cut in and leaving a small turning along

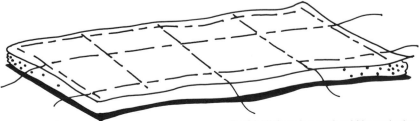

Fig 26 All three layers should be tacked together before working hand stitches

each edge (each piece of appliqué should be lapped over a previous one by this turning amount so that there are no gaps through which the base fabric will show). Draw in the straight grain on each traced piece so that the pieces, when appliquéd, will all be lying on the same grain. Appliqué the fabrics in sequence so that the base or background pieces of appliqué are worked first, with the topmost pieces applied last.

Hand Appliqué

Hand appliqué should be worked using a needle threaded with a strong sewing thread, similar in colour to the fabric being appliquéd. A blanket stitch should be worked over the raw edge, attaching it to the base fabric at the same time. The distance between each stitch will very much depend on the fabrics being appliquéd; blanket stitches worked very closely together (forming buttonhole stitch) look particularly effective on silks and shiny fabrics.

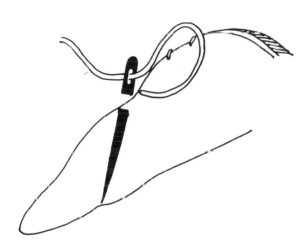

Fig 27 Slipstitch is used to hold the appliqué pieces to the base fabric when carrying out blind appliqué

Blind Appliqué

This is another hand method of appliqué and can be used if the appliqué fabrics have a tendency to fray and if a less stitched effect is desired. Each appliqué piece should have a small turning allowed on every edge. All edges that will show should be pressed to the wrong side and tacked in position before being appliquéd to the base fabric. If some of the edges are curved and seem difficult to turn to the wrong side, make little cuts within the turning allowance, to make the pressing and tacking easier. Place each appliqué section on the base fabric and slipstitch in place using a thread similar in colour to the fabric being appliquéd. Work each subsequent piece of appliqué in the same way.

Machine Appliqué

A quicker method than hand appliqué, machine appliqué gives a very professional finish to the work and is very durable.

It can be worked in one of two ways: with the presser foot attached using either machine satin stitch or a decorative stitch, or with the presser foot removed and the stitches worked with the free-machine embroidery technique. The second choice gives a more abstract feel to the design because the stitches are more random.

Whichever method you decide to use, each piece of appliqué should be tacked to the base fabric before machining. Small running stitches should be worked close to the raw edges in the thread to be used for the appliqué.

Using the presser-foot method, set the machine to a medium width zigzag stitch with a stitch length between 0 and 2, giving a closely worked machine satin stitch. If you have chosen a more decorative stitch, make sure the machine is set up so that the stitches are as wide as possible, with little space between them.

You may need to reduce the pressure on the foot a little so that the various layers of fabric run smoothly through the machine. Work the stitching along the raw edge of the piece to be appliquéd, keeping the centre of the presser foot in line with the raw edge – this will ensure that the stitching well covers the raw edge.

In a similar way, the machine is set for a closely worked satin stitch if you are going to experiment with the free-machine embroidery technique. Follow the directions given in the machine embroidery section for removing the presser foot and dropping the 'feed'. Because this type of machine work is more random and somewhat less controllable, experiment with scraps of fabric before starting the actual design.

As with any of the design techniques you may choose, the work will be more professionally finished if the stitching is worked with the base fabric stretched in a frame, be it a tambour or rectangular frame. This applies very much to machine or hand appliqué. Do note, however, that the pieces of appliqué should be tacked to the base fabric before the fabric is stretched in a frame to prevent puckering when the work is finally removed.

As you will see, some of the designs have included appliqué which is lightly padded. This gives a soft, raised effect that can bring some areas of your design out in relief. It is perhaps easier to produce this effect using hand appliqué as the section can be padded as you stitch. Use small pieces of terylene wadding placed underneath the appliqué piece, then tack and hand stitch this section securely to the work.

Canvas Work

Canvas work is embroidery worked on canvas, which distinguishes it from other forms of hand embroidery. The regularity of the canvas confines the stitch to a certain shape, with the use of threads and colour introducing the inspirational aspect of the technique. The complete piece could be worked in canvas work or alternatively, a small area could be completed and attached to a larger piece of work involving other design techniques.

The canvas forms the base fabric for the design; it is available in various qualities from most good needlecraft departments. Being an even-weave cloth, canvas is defined by the number of threads per inch – the more threads to an inch, the finer the canvas. The various qualities can be found in either single- or double-thread canvas (double-thread canvas is defined by the number of double threads per inch). But it is useful to note that single-thread canvas has greater possibilities than double-thread canvas, because only a handful of stitches can be worked on the latter.

Woollen threads are the obvious choice for canvas work, although stunning effects can be created with a subtle mix of stranded cottons, metallic threads, brilliant silks and soft matt cottons. It is very important that the thread you choose will cover the canvas well. If the thread you have chosen seems a little flat when worked on the canvas, the 'tramming' technique can be used to pad out the stitch and help it to stand proud of the canvas. Use a tapestry needle with a blunt end so that the needle passes easily through the canvas, and always use short lengths of thread as you work to prevent the length from twisting and getting worn by continuously being passed through the canvas holes.

The work, unless particularly small, should be attached to a roller-type frame to prevent the stitches from distorting. The tambour frame, in this instance, is most unsuitable: the canvas would become crushed when set between the two rings.

Plan your design on graph paper, counting each square on the paper as one stitch. Coloured crayons can be used to give an idea of thread colours and the way in which different colours work next to each other.

Areas of the design can then be redrawn onto the canvas before it is attached to the frame; alternatively, the graph-paper drawing can be referred to stitch by stitch, as you work.

The various stitches given below are those most commonly used – you can work just one or a combination.

Tramming

Tramming is a preparation stitch over which the actual stitch is worked. It helps to thicken up the stitch and to give the work a good surface texture.

Using the same thread as the stitch to be worked, bring the thread up from the back of the work, leaving the thread-end at the back. The stitches are worked horizontally over the single thread of canvas, or pairs of thread (known as 'tramlines'). Work in overlapping stitches, no more than 12cm (4¾in) long, starting each new stitch from the end of the last stitch. At the end of a row, take the thread through to the wrong side and work both the tramming ends into the back of the work as you stitch.

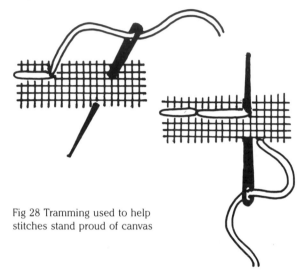

Fig 28 Tramming used to help stitches stand proud of canvas

Half-cross Stitch

This is a very popular stitch which can cover huge areas of canvas. It is worked from left to right and can work well stitched over prepared tramming stitches. Bring the thread up from the back of the work at the bottom left corner of the row to be stitched, then down through the next hole on the top right. Continue in this way, forming a slanted stitch on the front of the work and a straight stitch on the back. Run the ends of threads back through the wrong side of the work and cut off close to the work so that the back is kept neat and tidy. (See also Cross Stitch, page 17.)

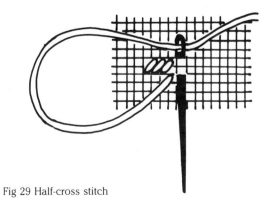

Fig 29 Half-cross stitch

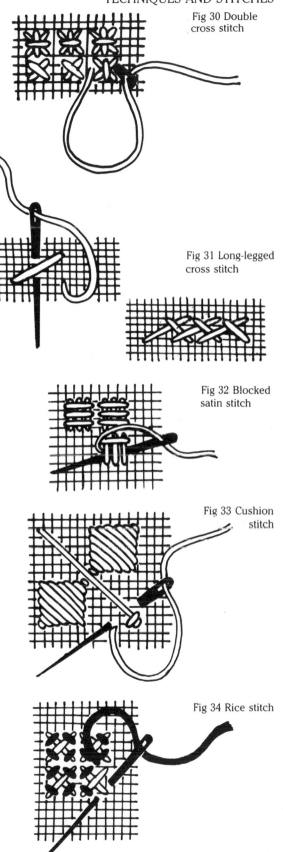

Fig 30 Double cross stitch

Fig 31 Long-legged cross stitch

Fig 32 Blocked satin stitch

Fig 33 Cushion stitch

Fig 34 Rice stitch

Double Cross Stitch

Work a single cross stitch as described in the hand-embroidery section, then bring the needle through to the right side between the lower ends of the crossed threads. Insert the needle between the top ends of the crossed threads and out again centrally to the left. Take the needle over the opposite side of the cross and centrally through to the wrong side. Bring it through to the right side at the position for the next stitch.

Long-legged Cross Stitch

This stitch is worked from left to right with the stitch being worked over several more threads of the canvas than the previous stitches. With the needle brought through to the right side of the canvas, take a long slanting stitch, bringing the needle out vertically a short distance below. Insert the needle above and halfway along the first slanted stitch, then bring it out vertically through the fabric, under the slanting stitch.

Blocked Satin Stitch

Three vertical straight stitches are covered by three horizontal straight stitches.

Cushion Stitch

Diagonal stitches are worked over the size of square required. When two squares are worked next to each other as shown in the diagram, a gap appears between them. This should be filled by a long tramming stitch taken the other way, which is then covered by the same cushion stitch.

Rice Stitch

Rice stitch is made up of rows of cross stitch over which bars of cross stitch are worked either in the same thread or in an alternative thread or colourway.

Once several stitches have been mastered, it is worthwhile experimenting with different-coloured threads in various colour sequences and combinations of a number of stitches worked together.

Rugwork

Rugwork is a highly textured design technique which can be used very effectively to create rugged areas of scenery. Janet Phillips adopted this idea in Rain Clouds over the Beacons, using a piece of rugwork to depict the foreground landscape. A variety of threads was used together with various rugging techniques for a field full of reality and charm. Rugging canvas is thicker than the regular canvas used for canvas work and for this reason, it does not have to be set in a frame. It also has larger holes, so it should be worked with thicker threads and yarns.

Tufted rug wool is now widely available and comes in a good range of shades. The short lengths of yarn are attached to the canvas with a rug hook, giving a deep-pile appearance with cut thread-ends.

Tapestry wool can also be used on rug canvas and can be used double or even treble, so that the holes of the canvas are completely covered. Wool can be combined with silks and cottons to give a highly textured feel. You can experiment with all the usual canvas-work stitches on rug canvas, although the half-cross stitch is probably the most successful.

If you want to attach a section of rugwork to an even bigger piece of work, the edges of the canvas should be neatened with an overcasting stitch worked in one of the yarns used in the work.

Spinning, Dyeing and Weaving

Designing and working a piece of embroidery can be taken a stage further still with the introduction of crafts such as spinning, weaving and dyeing. The base fabric, together with the yarns and colours you use, can all be made by you.

Heather de Backer, in her design Manx Morning, has created a most beautiful piece of work consisting of hand-woven woollen thread. The subtle blend of threads has been achieved by using wool hand-spun from the fleece of the Manx sheep then coloured superbly with natural vegetable dyes. This devotion to a craft obviously demands many hours of work even before the design and stitchery part are started. Do not, however, be put off by this as the resulting embroidery is so satisfying and will be no less than a work of art.

Spinning is a large subject to touch on, involving collecting the fleece as well as cleaning, preparing and spinning the yarn. If you are interested in using these techniques, a good book suggested in the bibliography will describe the various stages in detail.

The dyeing of natural yarn is also a very large subject. The ways in which natural fruits and vegetables, not to mention plants, can be used to create wonderful colours are limitless. Dyeing techniques should be studied carefully as the dyes need to be 'fixed' with the help of a mordant agent measured to precise quantities.

Weaving is the construction stage of a piece of work and does not have to involve expensive looms and equipment. It is an age-old craft carried through generations, from times when wood and yarn were the materials readily to hand. A simple frame can be constructed using this old principle and you can produce pieces of equal quality to those worked on an advanced loom.

Four pieces of wood should be fixed together with nails so that the pieces are at right angles to each other. It is important for the frame to be square so that the worked piece will be of a good, even shape. The next stage is to set up the warp threads which will form the threads running down the length of the work. These warp threads can be made from coton à broder or even fine string, as they will not show once the work has been completed. Set a row of flat-headed nails across the top and bottom edges of the frame so that they are in line with each other and between 3 and 10 mm (⅛ and ⅜ in) apart, depending on how firm or loose you want the work to be. Starting at the first nail on the top row, knot the end of the warp thread in position. Bring the warp thread down to the bottom row of nails and secure the thread tightly round the first nail so that the thread from top to bottom of the frame is good and taut. Leave a length of thread, cut off, then begin again at the next nail on the top row until all the warp threads have been completed.

A shuttle is required to hold the weft yarn, which can be anything from wool or cotton to narrow strips of fabric. A piece of wood or card can be cut and shaped into a shuttle that will make a very adequate tool for going in and out of the warp thread. Wind the weft thread round the shuttle, unwinding it as you work the piece. The shuttle should be passed under and over the warp threads, with the warp threads kept single or grouped into twos and threes, giving a longer stitch length. When you reach the end of the row, turn round and come back weaving in reverse, going over the warp threads which you previously went under and vice versa. After each row has been worked, make sure that the stitches are

Fig 35 A simple wooden frame showing the warp threads attached

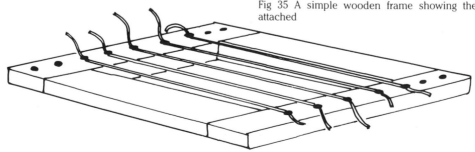

Fig 37 Casting on stitches

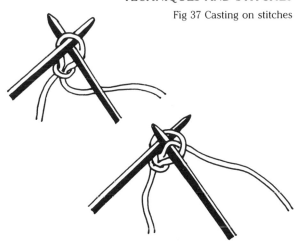

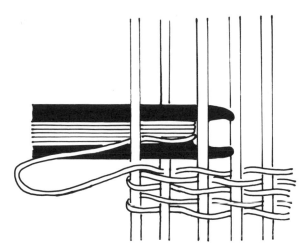

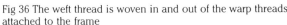

Fig 36 The weft thread is woven in and out of the warp threads attached to the frame

packed down firmly, with the warp threads concealed. A range of coloured threads can be introduced on the different rows or changed midway across a row (the ends should be secured neatly together on the wrong side of the work).

When the work is completed, remove the piece from the frame and knot the warp ends in groups to form decorative tassels. The top ends of the warp threads can be neatened round a pole or bamboo stick to form a wall-hanging.

Knitting

Knitting is another textural medium you may like to use, either as the complete idea for your design or as a section of texture to highlight an area of your work. It is a very varied and interesting craft, including a wealth of wonderful stitches and yarn textures. Without getting too heavily into the subject, several stitches can be learnt and used to great effect; the easiest of these are garter stitch and stocking stitch, which are both based on the same method of construction.

Casting On

Casting on a row is the first step in knitting and forms the base for the subsequent rows. There are several methods to follow for this, the easiest perhaps being the thumb method. First make a slip loop by forming a circle with the yarn and drawing a loop from the ball through this circle. Place the loop on the needle as the first stitch.

To cast on stitches, hold the yarn from the ball in the right hand and the loose end of the yarn in the left. Form a loop on the left thumb.

Place the point of the right-hand needle into the loop and with the right hand wrap the yarn round the point of the needle and draw through the loop on the thumb. Slip the loop off the thumb, tightening the left-hand thread at the same time.

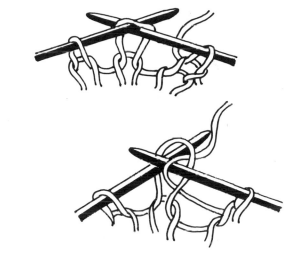

Fig 38 Basic knit stitch

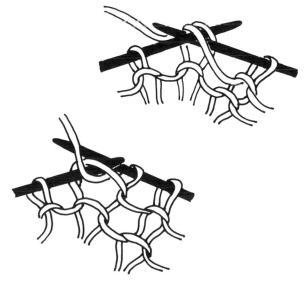

Fig 39 Basic purl stitch

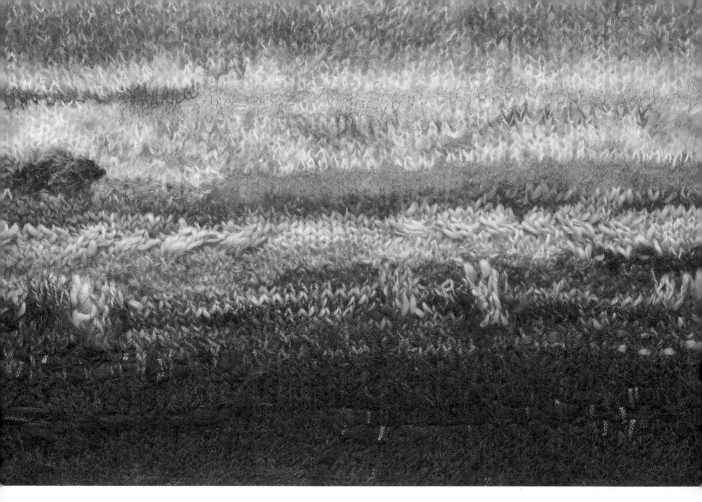

This Green and Pleasant Land, which uses simple knitting techniques plus surface embroidery, see page 99

Continue in this way until the required number of stitches has been cast on.

Garter Stitch
Garter stitch is made up of continuous rows of knit stitch. Insert the point of the right-hand needle into the first stitch on the left-hand needle. Bring working yarn over right-hand needle point and draw loop through.

Stocking Stitch
Stocking stitch is based on one row of knit and one row of purl. Follow the instructions given above for the knit row, then purl a row. The same method is followed, except that you purl into the back of the strand that has been slipped on the point of the left-hand needle instead of knitting into the back of it.

Casting Off
Casting off is usually carried out on a knit row and gives a finished edge to the knitting. Knit the first two stitches and insert point of left-hand needle into first stitch. Lift first stitch over the second and off needle. Knit next stitch and continue to lift one stitch over another in the same way. Casting off on a purl row is carried out the same way with the stitches being purled instead of knitted.

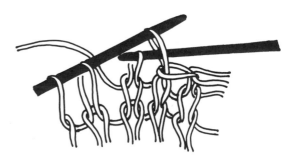

Fig 39a Casting off

4
Finishing and Mounting

The finishing and mounting of your work is as important as the quality of the hand work used to create the design. Many a piece can be enhanced or ruined by the way in which it is mounted.

When the work has been completed, make sure all the thread ends are secure on the wrong side and check that no stitching has been left out during construction.

If the work has been set in a tambour or rectangular frame, it will need to be pressed to present a good, flat surface for mounting. Work should never be pressed on the right side for fear of causing the threads and fabrics to shine or the textural stitches and techniques to flatten. Place the work face downwards on several layers of blanket covered with a clean white sheet. Lay another piece of fabric over the wrong side of the work and press very lightly, using a little steam if necessary (do not use steam if silk has been appliquéd, as water does tend to mark it). If your work has become slightly distorted during construction, pin the piece out on the blanket so that the shape is correct, then press in the same way. Before setting about choosing a mount or frame, decide where you are going to place the work. Look at the surrounding decor. Are the walls plain or patterned? What is the overall colour of the room? What style are the ornaments, and are you creating a nostalgic or modern setting? All these questions should be answered to determine the style and look into which you are going to introduce your design. There are several methods for presenting your work, possibly the most obvious being to mount it in a picture frame.

Many designers and craftswomen prefer to have their work framed by a specialist framer as this does give the finished piece an added touch of professionalism. A frame does help to keep the work clean and in some instances prolongs its life. The many framing companies will advise you on the colour and size of the mounting board, together with the size and type of frame.

Home-made frames can be attempted with the help of a mitre block, angle clamps and a fine saw. You may find, though, that the choice of framing materials available in retail ranges is not as extensive as those found in framing shops.

If you have a liking for antiques or nostalgia, an old frame will fit well in your interior scheme. Many an old frame can be renovated and cleaned with surprisingly good results. The cleaning of the wood can be simply done with a fine wire wool soaked in white spirit. Work the wire wool into the wooden frame, following the grain of the wood to prevent irregular scratches. Very thick paint or varnish must be removed with a paint stripper. Smooth down any splinters of wood with sandpaper, then apply several coats of varnish or paint. You might like to give the frame one of the more modern paint treatments which are becoming increasingly popular – these include ragging, stencilling or sponging and give subtle, dappled paint effects.

Mounting

The following method of mounting work is encouraged by many embroidery groups and institutions because the embroidery, with its variety of colour and texture, can be clearly seen and even felt. A piece of board or card is cut to the finished size of the work; the design is mounted onto this with the excess edges of the fabric secured firmly out of sight on the wrong side of the work. This can then, if desired, be mounted on a slightly larger board still, covered in the same base fabric or a complementary one.

This method is most suitable for square or rectangular shapes but not for highly textured designs that will pick up dirt easily.

Mounting Equipment

You will need:

Mounting board – the thickness of the board very much depends on the size of the work to be mounted. Thick card will be adequate for a small piece, with hardboard being more suitable for larger designs. It is a good idea to get the hardboard cut at a timber yard so that the edges are smooth and straight. Other boards such as blockboard, plywood and chipboard can be used, although they tend to be heavier than the same thickness of hardboard.

Craft or Stanley knife – fitted with a sharp blade.

Masking or hessian tape – for holding the edges of the fabric down to the wrong side of the mounting board.

Hammer and short tacks – for securing fabric in position if glue is not strong enough.

Hanging cord, picture hook and screw eyes.

Adhesive – use a good, strong adhesive that can be applied sparingly and dries to a clear finish.

Mounting the Work

1 If the base fabric of the work is particularly thin, cover the mounting board with a layer of cotton sheeting or lawn.

2 With the mounting board prepared and the work ironed flat, mark the centre position along all edges on both the work and the board.

3 Lay a cloth over a flat surface with the work face down on it. Place the board over the top with the centre marks of the board and work matching and the board centrally placed over the design.

4 Working with the shorter sides first, bring one edge of fabric over to the wrong side and stick down, making sure the fabric is carried tightly over the board edge. Leave the adhesive to set. Bring the other short end round to the wrong side, making sure again that the edges are taut, and stick in place. Leave these two sides to dry well.

5 Fold each of the corners in the same way, without cutting the fabric. A little of the excess fabric at each corner can be cut off if the layers are becoming too thick. With the corners folded, stick the other two sides in place, making sure all the time that the work is remaining square to the board, giving a neat, taut effect.

6 When the work has been mounted, the back of the board must be neatened in one of two ways: with a piece of fabric covering the entire back area, or with tape laid over the raw edges of the work and stuck in position. For the fabric

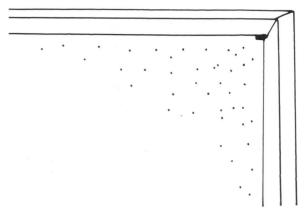

Fig 40 The excess fabric is taken round to the wrong side and stuck to the back of the mounting board with the corners neatly folded

method, cut out a piece of straight-grain fabric the size of the mounting board plus a good turning on all edges. Press the turnings to the wrong side and place over the mounted work with raw edges facing. Slipstitch the folded edge of the backing cloth to the edges of the work using a strong thread and small stitches. Attach two small curtain rings parallel to the top edge of the work on the wrong side. Thread a piece of cord between the two rings for hanging. The tape method is equally suitable. Cut two pieces of tape to the length and width of the mounted work. Place the two longer pieces over the turnings on the wrong side, with the tape placed centrally to the raw edge. Tack and slipstitch the outer edges of these tapes securely in place, again using a strong thread and small stitches. Stick down the inner edges of these two tapes. Repeat this process with the two shorter lengths

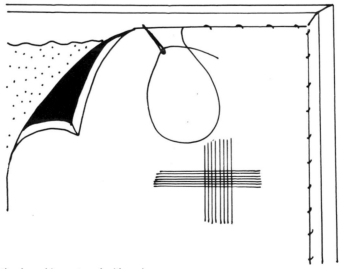

Fig 41 The back of the mounting board is neatened with a piece of fabric slipstitched in place

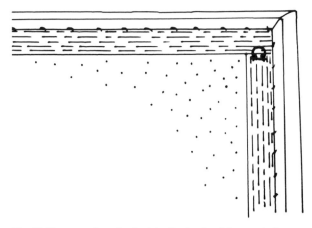

Fig 42 Tape can be attached to the back of the work for an equally good method of finishing off the wrong side of the mounting board

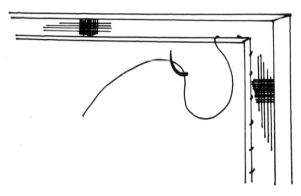

Fig 43 One mounting board is slipstitched to another, creating a double-mount effect

of tape, allowing the glue to dry well at each stage. Sew two small curtain rings parallel to the top edge through which a piece of cord can be threaded for hanging.

A double mount is yet another variation, with the mounted work set onto a second mount board. The second, slightly larger board forms a border to the design work and, depending on the fabric used, can enhance the colours of fabrics and thread used in the design. Following the method given for covering a mounting board, cover the smaller board with the work and the larger one with the same base fabric or a complementing one. Neaten the back of both boards using the tape method for the board mounted with the work. Place the one over the other, so that the same amount of the second mounting board is showing around all edges. Using a large tacking stitch, secure each corner of the work to the larger mount. Each edge of the work should then be slipstitched in place using a strong thread and very small, almost invisible stitches. You will probably find a curved glove needle useful when working these particular stitches. Stitch curtain rings to the wrong side of the larger mount to take the hanging cord.

If you are at all unsure about mounting your work, do consider having the work professionally mounted. Hours of loving work should be given the treatment it deserves.

To retain the density of colour that new fabrics and threads have, make sure the work is not placed in direct sunlight under which the colours are likely to fade.

(*overleaf*) The Laburnum Arch in Bodnant Garden, see page 36

The Designs

The Laburnum Arch in Bodnant Garden

The scene is worked entirely in free-machine embroidery on a painted background. The tree-trunks are densely satin stitched and blocks of satin stitch illustrate the delicate laburnum flowers and foliage. All types of machine threads are used to achieve the best blend of colour and texture. (Colour photograph pages 34–5.)

Materials

Cream cotton fabric – 35 × 45cm (13¾ × 17¾in).

Machine-embroidery threads in shades of lemon, yellow and gold, light green, mid-green and dark green, khaki, ochre, mid-brown and dark browns, soft and dark green-blues, soft turquoise, pale and bright pinks and cerise.

Transfer paints (see Stockists).

Embroidery ring – 20cm (7⅞in) in diameter.

Making Up the Design

1 Following Fig 44, mark out the design in the centre of a piece of paper cut to the same size as the finished work (note that the design will be reversed when the paints are transferred from the paper to the fabric). Using the transfer paints, paint the background areas onto the paper, keeping the colours very soft and muted and allowing them to merge into each other. Use pale green for tree foliage and yellow where the flowers are palest. Paint the area below the foliage soft turquoise. Paint the bushes soft green with very dull pink on the flowery areas. Paint the side of the path a dull blue-grey and the path khaki. Transfer the finished paintwork to the fabric following instructions on bottle.

2 Insert the area being stitched in the embroidery ring very tautly and reposition the ring as required. For stitch instructions, see Chapter 3. Working from the right side, stitch tree-trunks and lower branches in satin stitch, using dark-brown threads on near trees and slightly lighter shades on more distant trees. Build up a rounded depth of stitching on the thicker trunks. Highlight the fore-edges of near trees at left of arch with narrow, mid-brown zigzag stitching.

3 The foliage areas are stitched in random blocks of vertical zigzag stitching. Tighten top tension and loosen bobbin tension so long loops of underthread are pulled through to the right side. Use a wide stitch at the top and at either side of the picture and gradually reduce width as stitching recedes along the arch. Blend colours subtly by intermixing shades in top and bobbin thread and using a variety of yellow and green shades. Vary density of stitching, allowing background to show through.

4 Stitch darker areas of foliage in browns and ochres; space the stitching so greens can be added into these areas. Work some stitches over tree-trunks so they blend into the foliage. At top left corner intermix dark green and light green with a little yellow over the brown stitching. Working towards the right, use less dark green and add in more bright light greens, golds and yellow. At left foreground work downwards, through mixed greens and yellows, to soft green, then brighter yellows, to finish with lemon at lower edge of foliage. Work rest of foliage using softer shades as stitching recedes along arch.

5 Work area below foliage in random straight stitching in a soft turquoise. Space stitching widely so plenty of background shows through.

6 Work the green and pink bushes in the same way but stitch a little more densely. Work bushes in mid-greens, and flowers in intermixed pale and bright pinks. Use stronger colours in the foreground, shading into softer colours as stitching recedes along arch.

7 Stitch area between edge of path and trees. Using a warm, dark-brown thread, define the edge of the path with a few rows of straight stitching, then work towards the trees with random straight stitching; change colours from brown to khaki, then to pale green, to finish at base of trees.

8 Stitch path in a dull brown thread. Straight stitch from edge of path towards centre, then back to edge. Stitch densely at sides of path and space stitching widely at centre.

9 Stitch bush to left of path at far end fairly

densely in random straight stitches. Use dark-green threads highlighted by pulling through a small amount of turquoise underthread to the right side. Stitch small green areas beyond end of arch in soft-green random straight stitches.

10 Stitch bush to right foreground densely in random straight stitches. Use dark emerald-green and bright-green top threads with a bright cerise underthread pulled through to the right side.

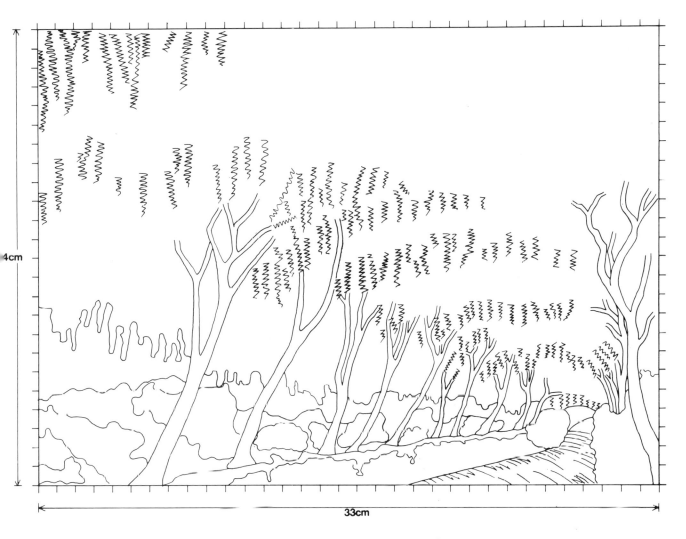

Fig 44 Diagram of The Laburnum Arch in Bodnant Garden

C. BALLS

A Roman Bridge

The ancient bridge, depicted in blocks of satin stitch, is set amid a rolling countryside. The gentle undulations of the land are described perfectly by Cretan stitch, and bullion stitch adds more texture to the tree and bush in the foreground. (Colour photograph opposite.)

Materials

Even-weave cotton – 35 × 45cm (13¾ × 17¼in).
Stranded cotton in shades of pale blue, three shades of mid- to dark blue, shades of green, brown and ochre, plus gold, cream, white, lemon and beige.
Embroidery frame – 30 × 40cm (11¾ × 15¾in).

Making Up the Design

1 Following Fig 45 and referring to Transferring Your Design onto Fabric (Chapter 1), mark out the design centrally on fabric and attach fabric to embroidery frame. Divide stranded cotton and use three threads together throughout. For stitch instructions, see Chapter 3.
2 Work tree in mid-browns using satin stitch for trunk and bigger branches and stem stitch for smaller branches. Outline left side of trunk and branches in dark-brown stem stitch. Work leaves in closely packed, dark-green bullion stitch.
3 Work sky in horizontal rows of stem stitch, intermixing pale-blue thread and white thread.

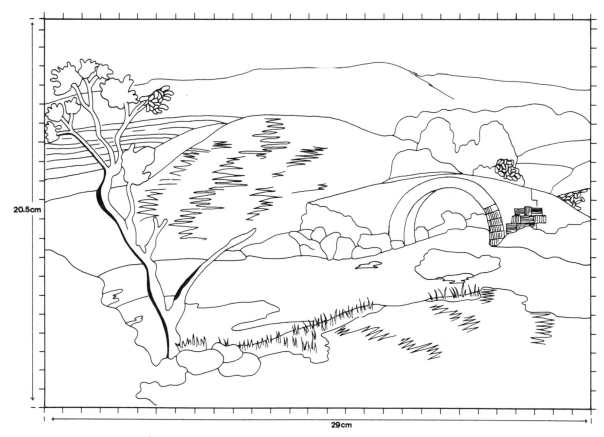

20.5cm

29cm

Fig 45 Diagram of A Roman Bridge

4 Stitch background hills in rows of dark-brown stem stitch, curving the lines of stitching to follow the outline of the hills.

5 Work area at left below the brown hills with couched threads in stripes of cream and gold, and cream and soft green. Fill in area below stripes in pale-green satin stitches, spaced at random.

6 Stitch the central hill and mid-green area below the stripes in Cretan stitch. Working from the top towards the bottom, gently zigzag the stitching from side to side as you work. Overlap rows to fill in the area densely, and intermix a few areas worked in ochre, gold, lemon and pale green on the central hill.

7 Work bushes behind the hedge in dark green, pale greens and ochre, using Cretan stitch worked sideways. Fill in the pale- and mid-green fields on the right in couching and stem stitch.

8 Outline top of bridge in dark-brown stem stitch. Highlight top of bridge at the left with rows of stem stitch in lemon and then gold above the brown. Work yellow areas above the bridge in bullion stitch using shades of lemon, gold and ochre.

9 Using mid-brown, stitch arch of bridge in blocks of satin stitch radiating out from the arch. Fill in main part of bridge in blocks of vertical and horizontal satin stitch worked in mid-brown with a cream area to the right. Stitch shadow under arch in dark-brown satin stitch.

10 Stitch rocks along river edge in satin stitches worked at different angles for each rock in shades of beige and light brown. Work rock in river in long-and-short satin stitch in shades of dark and mid-brown with dark brown at the base.

11 Fill in remaining areas on far bank with Cretan stitch worked sideways and intermixing mid-green, lemon and ochre. Add random bullion stitches to these areas in the same colours.

12 Work river in gently curving rows of stem stitch in shades of dark, mid- and pale blue. Fill in near bank, using Cretan stitch in the same way as on the hills in shades of mid- and dark green with an ochre area near river. Add dark-green reeds in straight stitch along the river bank.

13 Fill in bush at left foreground with closely packed bullion stitches worked in dark green with a few areas of mid-green and random lemon stitches as highlights.

JANE GREWCOCK

Cottage of Gaddesby

A very small intricate design, worked almost entirely in tiny straight stitches which mix and blend colours with great subtlety to create very delicate and realistic textures. (Colour photograph on page 14.)

Materials

Fine even-weave cream cotton – 30cm (11¾in) square.

Stranded cotton in shades of green from light to dark and from bright to dull, shades of brown from tan to dark, three toning shades of beige, two close shades of dark grey, pale blue, plus small amounts of white, black, cream, lilac and red.

Embroidery ring – 20cm (7⅞in) in diameter.

Making Up the Design

1 Following Fig 46, and referring to Transferring Your Design onto Fabric (Chapter 1), mark out the design on the centre of the fabric and insert in embroidery ring. Divide threads and use a single strand throughout. For stitch instructions, see Chapter 3.

2 Using grey thread, begin at lower edge of near roof. Work a row of small (about 3mm (⅛in) long) straight stitches across roof, following the line of the lower edge. Work a second line close to the first, overlapping ends of stitches so that they do not finish at the same place. Complete roof in this way, intermixing the two shades of grey.

3 Stitch grey part of far roof in the same way. Stitch top half of front of far house in the same way, using tan thread and adding a few tiny stitches in darker brown below the window.

4 Stitch side of far house with 1–2mm (¹⁄₁₆–⅛in) long straight stitches, intermixing cream, beige and tan stitches at random with a few grey ones.

5 Stitch lower part of far chimney in the same way, using darker stitches to outline front corner. Stitch top part of chimney in the same way, adding in a few black stitches. Work chimney-pot in vertical tan stitches with two black stitches across the top.

6 Work brickwork on side of near house at the top, bottom and over the area covered by branches beside the window with horizontal lines of couched thread. Intermix tan and grey with a little cream, using two strands together for the couched thread and a single strand of grey for the vertical fastening-down stitches. Pack lines densely and stitch fairly closely together. Stitch chimney in the same way, with a row of cream near the top.

7 Work near window in vertical grey couching with a cream strip at the right-hand side. Fill in window on front of far house with white couching. Outline window frames in white and top right-hand corner of far window in black.

8 Working horizontally, stitch pale-blue sky area in the same way as roof. In the same way, fill in the road area near the houses with stitches parallel to the houses in the medium shade of beige. Outline this with a border of the darker beige. Then fill in the remaining road area in the pale beige.

9 Stitch the tree-trunk in small vertical stitches, intermixing medium and dark browns. Stitch branches in the same way. Work twigs and leaves on both tall trees with tiny stitches at different angles, but generally following the line of the branches. Use shades of dark green and brown.

10 Work bushes in front of trees in the same way but using different shades of dark green and mostly vertical stitches. Stitch a portion of the bright green bush in the same way. Work bushes behind trees in two different shades of lighter green, with a darker shade at the bottom; stitch mostly at horizontal angles.

11 Stitch top of porch in grey straight stitches outlined in black. Stitch porch with vertical stitches in bright green, and criss-crossed stitches at the side for lattice work.

12 Stitch climbing plant at far end of near house with tiny stitches at different angles in pale and mid-greens. Next to that, stitch the darker climbing plant in the same way, intermixing dark green, brown and tan, and shading into dark greens only at near corner of house.

13 Work branches on the window wall in dark-brown straight stitches. Then fill in leaves in pale and mid-greens in the same way as before, but allowing the brickwork to show through around the branches.

14 Fill in bushes in foreground with tiny stitches in shades of bright and dull green. Stitch bush in front of house and grasses in bright light greens; stitch flowers in red and lilac.

15 Work corner of distant house in white with the roof outlined in tan. Stitch gate in foreground with long stitches in dark beige, using six strands of thread.

16 Accentuate top corner and front edge of roof on near house with a fine line of black straight stitches. Repeat this detail on far house.

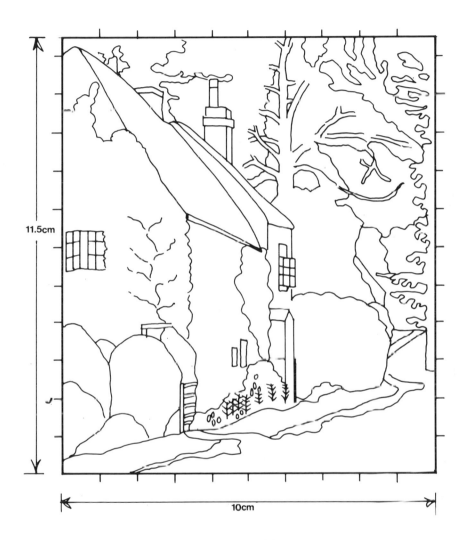

Fig 46 Diagram of Cottage of Gaddesby

EDITH BURLISON

Cornish Fishing Village

This heavily textured view of a fishing boat in Mevagissey harbour is surprisingly simple, but very effective. It is worked in a combination of appliqué and satin stitch, with the application of unusual materials such as plastic mesh and a drinking straw. (Colour photograph opposite).

Materials

White backing cloth – 40 × 50cm (15¾ × 19⅝in).
Blue-green and blue-grey chiffon, each piece 14 × 26cm (5½ × 10¼in).
Blue lining fabric – 18 × 26cm (7 × 10¼in).
Green lining fabric – 13 × 26cm (5⅛ × 10¼in).
Stranded cotton in dark, medium and pale grey, terracotta, dark, mid- and light brown, white and black.
Tapestry wools in shades of dull and mid-greens.
Embroidery silk in beige and white.
Thin cord in gold, black and gold mixed, and grey for boat and rigging.
Scrap of synthetic wadding.
Strip of sage-green suede – 1.5 × 26cm (½ × 10¼in).
Oddment of sage-green fabric.
Plastic mesh in greens and oranges (as used for fruit and vegetable bags)
Drinking straw.
Fabric paints.
Fabric adhesive.
Embroidery ring – 30cm (11¾in) in diameter.

Making Up the Design

1 Following Fig 47, draw design on tracing paper. Lightly mark out the buildings centrally on the white backing cloth, following Chapter 1, Transferring Your Design onto Fabric. Cut the blue lining to the shape of the sky, finishing just below the foliage area. Spread adhesive roughly over blue lining. Attach wadding and leave to dry. When dry, pull off most of wadding, leaving a wispy cloud effect. Apply a little grey paint in between the wadding to give the sky a stormy appearance. Cover sky area with blue-grey chiffon turning top and side edges under lining and hand stitching in place to base cloth. Set work in embroidery ring and begin working stitching. For stitch instructions, see Chapter 3.

2 Using satin stitch embroider buildings; work the fronts of the buildings in a variety of white, grey and light-brown stranded cotton, using three strands at a time. Use the satin stitch vertically, horizontally and diagonally to give the buildings variety in depth and texture.

3 Work the roofs of the buildings in the same way using dark brown, dark grey, terracotta and a touch of white; work the window areas in colours to contrast with the buildings. Outline the windows in straight stitch, using a single strand of black thread and work cross stitch over the windows to give the appearance of frames.

4 Fill in foliage between buildings and sky with French knots worked in the various shades of green tapestry wool. Remove work from ring.

5 Tack the green lining to the sea area, cutting it away at base of buildings. Paint the reflection of the buildings on the green lining, using muted shades of the colours of the buildings. Cover sea area with blue-green chiffon, turning the base and side edges under the lining and hand stitching in place to base fabric.

6 Lay the strip of suede across work to form harbour wall and secure in place with a few vertical stitches worked over the suede in brown stranded cotton.

7 Cut out base of boat in sage-green fabric and slipstitch in position. Work a deep band of vertical satin stitch along base of boat, using two strands of white cotton. Work the front and top edges of the boat in black satin stitch.

8 Using a variety of brown and terracotta stranded cottons and two strands, complete bow and cabin of boat in satin stitch. Work French knots in beige embroidery silk to the right of the cabin to resemble nets, and hand sew a length of gold cord just below the top; satin stitch edge of the boat to accentuate the shape.

9 Cut the drinking straw to a 16cm (6¼in) length and wind light-brown stranded cotton over its entire length. Secure it to the work as the boat's mast, using a few large stitches in the same thread.

10 Embroider top rigging using long stitches of white embroidery silk. Work the rest of rigging in beige embroidery silk and black and gold mixed cord, taking very long stitches so that the thread lies proud of the work. Attach a length of grey cord as a cross rigging just above the cabin and a black and gold cord mooring rope from the base of the boat into the sea.

11 Screw up small pieces of plastic mesh and attach to the lower left-hand corner with several hand stitches. Dab the mesh with green, brown and orange paint to make it look well used.

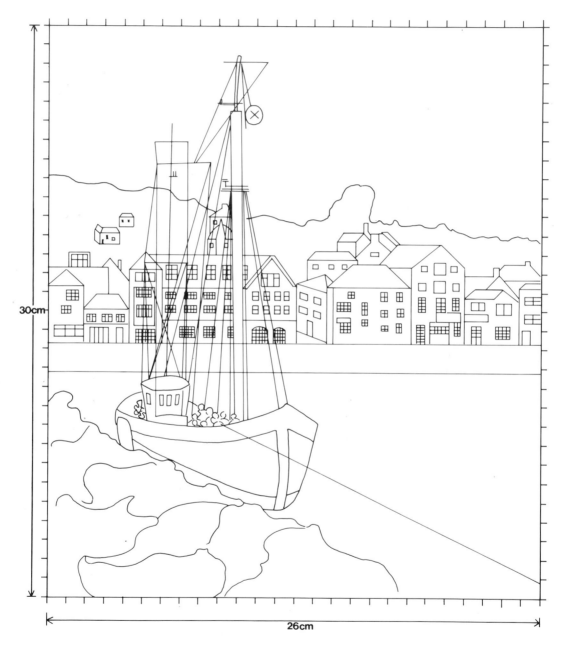

Fig 47 Diagram of Cornish Fishing Village

A Peace of Yorkshire

A cleverly worked piece taking in canvas work, appliqué and hand stitching. Padding is placed behind the canvas work to bring this area out to the forefront of the design. (Colour photograph page 47.)

Materials

Dark-blue base fabric – 30 × 50cm (11¾ × 19⅝in).
Green towelling – 15 × 30cm (6 × 11¾in).
Fine single canvas – 20 × 30cm (7⅞ × 11¾in).
Scraps of nylon netting in pale blue and brown plus a small piece of dark-brown netting.
Stranded cotton in dull and bright greens, brown, tan, beige, cream, black and orange.
Sewing threads in green and blue.
Thick wire.
Watercolours.

Making Up the Design

1 Following Fig 48, work the piece of canvas work to be used in the centre of the design. For stitch instructions, see Chapter 3. Follow the key given for the colours of threads to be used and work the piece using all six strands of the cotton and half cross stitch. To finish, use a single strand of cream stranded cotton worked in a criss-cross way over the black window areas.

2 Following Fig 48a, showing the general design lines, cut out the strip of towelling to be placed above and below the canvas work. Fold the meeting edge of each piece of towelling to the wrong side and slipstitch neatly to the last row of the canvas work so that the threads of the canvas are not visible.

3 This piece of work is mounted on the base fabric which is folded in several places to give the work a raised feel (it gives the same effect as wadding but with a more rigid appearance). Place the work over the base fabric, making folds in the base fabric at the top of the towelling section, at the start of the canvas work and at the top of the base towelling section. Tack the layers together around the outside edges to hold the work in place.

4 Place a strip of brown netting over the top area of towelling and machine the lower edge in position using a narrow, fairly closely worked zigzag stitch. Place a pale-blue netting over the base fabric above this, taking it to the top of the work. With blue thread and the same machine stitch, attach the lower edge of the netting to the base fabric. Fold a strip of the pale-blue netting in half and invisibly sew the fold of the netting in position with the two layers lying flat to the top of the work. Machine a line of blue straight stitching over the darker blue sky area in a curved line, to give this area some contour.

5 Using a single strand of dark-green stranded cotton, work French knots over the area of

Fig 48 Diagram of canvas work for A Peace of Yorkshire

□	cream and olive green together	×	mole brown
•	leaf green	∧	tan and beige together
⊙	brown and beige together	▽	orange and brown together
\	black	▲	white
v	pale olive green		

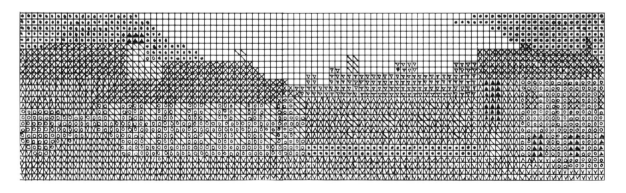

green stitching to the right of the canvas work. Carry the French knots down onto the towelling to form the base of the bush.

6 Curve a length of wire to the shape of the tree and wind cream and brown thread around its entire length. Additional branches can be attached as the thread is wound round and held in position by the thread. Catch the wire base to the left-hand side of the work, using a single strand of cream thread. Cut a piece of dark-brown netting to the shape of the top of the tree and spread glue over one side. Leave to dry and when hard, work chain stitch randomly over the netting, using a single strand of dark-green stranded cotton. Place this piece over the top area of the wire tree and work the same stitches over the edge of the netting to secure it to the work.

7 Using a variety of green threads and six strands together, work French knots in random groups over the base of the canvas work, occasionally taking the stitches over onto the towelling.

8 Mix some various green colours using the watercolours and paint a dark shade over the foreground of the work. Use the paint sparingly with a dabbing action so that the paint is absorbed by the towelling. Use a lighter green paint on the area of towelling just below the building on the left of the canvas work.

9 Using three strands of cotton and short and long straight stitches, work clumps of stitches to the bottom left-hand corner of the work.

10 Work a deep trunk of hand satin stitch just below bush on right of work using two strands of cotton. Give the appearance of a guard around this bush by using a long stitch and a single strand of stranded black cotton.

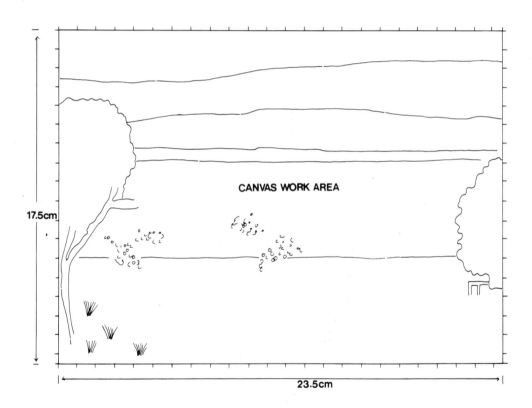

Fig 48a Diagram of A Peace of Yorkshire

A Peace of Yorkshire
A Royal Retreat

46

A Royal Retreat

Balmoral Castle is worked almost entirely in satin stitch. The sky and grass are stitched horizontally in fine thread to emphasise the strong blocks of vertical stitching which form the castle. (Colour photograph page 47.)

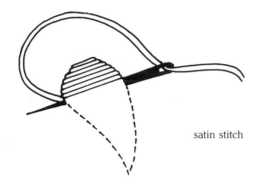

satin stitch

Materials
Even-weave linen – 40 × 50cm (15¾ × 19⅝in).
Stranded cotton in shades of pale blue, grey, beige and cream plus white and shaded blue for the sky; shades of beige, brown, grey, ochre and dull green for the castle and road; shades of green, brown and ochre for the grass and trees.
Embroidery frame – 30 × 40cm (11¾ × 15¾in).

Making Up the Design
1 Following Fig 49 and referring to Transferring Your Design onto Fabric (Chapter 1), mark out the design centrally on fabric and attach the fabric to the embroidery frame. For stitch instructions, see Chapter 3.
2 Divide cotton and use a single thread for the sky. Working areas of beige, cream, grey and white, stitch the clouds. Make horizontal satin stitches about 5 to 8mm (¼ to ⅜in) long; vary the length of each stitch slightly so that the edges are feathered. Follow the outline of the shape being filled in to give a gentle, undulating row of stitching. Stitch a second row next to the first in the same way, overlapping and feathering in the stitches where they meet so that there is no distinct line between the rows. Complete clouds. Work sky in the same way using shades of pale blue at the top and

intermixing areas of shaded blue thread and white in lower part of sky.
3 Use two strands of thread worked together for castle. Stitch the outlines on front of building in brown using straight stitch and stem stitch, and bands of satin stitch on the wider lines.
4 Stitch castle front in beige using vertical satin stitch. On smaller areas stitch blocks of one stitch and on larger areas feather in the stitches randomly where they meet.
5 Work roofs in shades of brown. Stitch the long, lowest roof in three rows of vertical satin stitch, and satin stitch the gables in grey with ochre fronts. Stitch other roofs in blocks of horizontal satin stitch.
6 Satin stitch chimneys in blocks of dull-green horizontal stitching, working bands of brown vertical satin stitch above this and finish with horizontal beige straight stitches at the top of each chimney.
7 Work tower on left in shades of brown horizontal satin stitch, and the castellations in beige vertical stitching. Stitch top of tower in blocks of dull-green satin stitching with a band of beige, and a beige pole with a grey cross on the top. Work grey crosses in the same way on the two sides of the tower.
8 On tower to the right, work turrets in blocks of dull-green horizontal satin stitch. Work castellations in vertical beige satin stitch, and spires and flagpole in dull-green horizontal stitching.
9 Fill in the two larger windows on tower by weaving six strands of grey thread under and over each other. Fill in all other windows and doors in blocks of satin stitch in greys and beige. Fill in other areas of brickwork with blocks of satin stitch in shades of brown.
10 Stitch tree-trunks in brown satin stitch and branches in stem stitch. Stitch leaves in shades of green using a single strand of the thread in rows of curving, close blanket stitch working from trunks and branches outwards.
11 Using two strands, work bushes below tree in random green satin stitch. Add areas of French knots in ochre. Work other bushes along front of buildings in dark-green French knots using three or four strands of thread.

12 Using a single strand of green thread, work grass in the same way as the sky. Using three strands of thread in three shades of darker green, straight stitch tufts and stem stitch lines on grass.

13 Work road in vertical satin stitch, using two strands of beige thread. Begin stitching along left side of road and work in bands, allowing some stitches to form into blocks of uneven depth and feather in other stitches with the next row.

14 Using two strands of thread, stitch wall in front of castle in dull-brown vertical satin stitch and archway in dark-beige horizontal satin stitch. Fill in archways with grey satin stitch. Using a single strand of dark beige, work blocks of horizontal satin stitch along path in front of building on left.

20.5cm

28cm

Fig 49 Diagram of A Royal Retreat

BARBARA WATSON

Autumn Glory in Lakeland

This lakeland scene has a very delicate texture. Cable stitch is used for most of the background, the water and foreground, and the same stitch is worked sideways to depict the slate roofs. The tree-trunks are smoothly rounded in satin stitch and crunchy French knots form the leaves. (Colour photograph opposite).

Materials

Even-weave linen – 25 × 30cm (9⅞ × 11¾in).
Stranded cotton in pale grey, silver grey, mid-grey, beige, bright tan, ochre, copper, brown, peach, dark green, two dull greens, khaki, apple green and white, plus small amounts of black, red, teal blue and pale turquoise.
Embroidery ring – 20cm (7⅞in) diameter.

Making Up the Design

1 Following Fig 50 and referring to Transferring Your Design onto Fabric (Chapter 1), mark out the design on the centre of the fabric and insert in embroidery ring. Divide thread and use two strands together throughout. For stitch instructions, see Chapter 3.

2 Work sky in rows of pale-grey cable stitch. Stitch horizontally, continuing over the areas where the French knots on trees will be stitched later, but not over the parts depicting branches.

3 Cable stitch dark-green areas at top of distant hills and at left of picture. Work stitching behind areas of French knots but not on the branches, and extend lower edge of stitching along shoreline to boats.

4 Fill in the trees on far shore in copper, ochre, tan and dull-green cable stitch. Then fill in the remaining area in dull-green and khaki cable stitch.

5 Work the tree to the right in copper-coloured stitching. Work small clumps of straight stitches with stitches beginning at the same base point and fanning out at the top. Stitch the clumps densely and pack them tightly together.

6 Stitch the dark-green tree at left foreground in

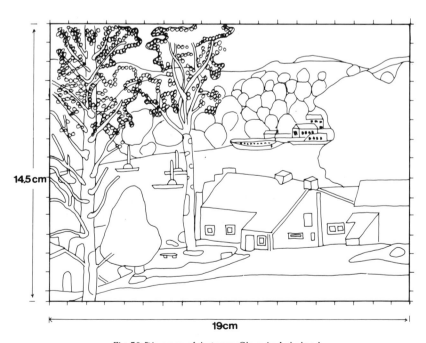

14.5cm

19cm

Fig 50 Diagram of Autumn Glory in Lakeland

the same way as the copper-coloured tree. Satin stitch trunk in black.

7 Work walls of buildings in the right foreground in beige cable stitch. Stitch bands of satin stitch along the ridges of roofs on both houses in silver grey and the gable ends in white.

8 Fill in main roof and roof of small outbuilding in silver-grey cable stitch, aligning the stitching with slope of roof. Stitch other roof to right with vertical cable stitch in silver grey.

9 Stitch chimneys in blocks of mid-grey satin stitch. Fill in doors and pipes in teal-blue satin stitch. Outline windows in white satin stitch and fill in their centres in pale-turquoise satin stitch. Satin stitch tiny window in white.

10 Stitch house to left in same way, but use mid-grey for walls and satin stitch roof in pale grey. Satin stitch mid-grey areas to right of house around tree-trunk.

11 Using cable stitch, fill in the ochre areas running from lower left corner towards centre house. Fill in the small areas under green tree in beige. Stitch area between green tree and

house, and foreground areas, in apple green.

12 Working from behind tree, satin stitch a band across lower edge of centre house to forecourt in mid-grey. Fill in forecourt in mid-grey cable stitch, aligning stitching with edges of apple-green areas.

13 Fill in remaining small areas on foreground: rock in water in teal-blue satin stitch, seats under tree in black satin stitch, and dark-green bush at right of picture in dark-green straight stitches.

14 Satin stitch tree-trunks in peach, then add brown patches. Work top branches and side branches in brown satin stitch. Stitch scattered, bright tan-coloured French knots around tree-tops to give the appearance of leaves.

15 Stitch houses on far shore in satin stitch with white walls, black windows and silver-grey roofs. Stitch shadow area behind building in forefront in mid-grey cable stitch.

16 Stitch boats in satin stitch following colours shown in photograph. Fill in water area in pale-grey cable stitch.

51

English Cornfield

The background of this free-machine embroidered scene is spray-painted to give strong, dense colour. The corn and grasses are worked in a bold sideways zigzag stitch, and thick perlé thread adds texture and lustre to the framing foliage. The scene is worked on very stiff fabric to eliminate the need for an embroidery ring. (Colour photograph page 23.)

Materials

Stiff roller-blind fabric or shirt-collar stiffening – 30 × 35cm (11¾ × 13¾in).

Size 16 machine needle.

Sewing thread, No 40, in shades of dark green, dull and bright greens, lemon, mid-yellow, gold and soft orange, plus small amounts of red, black and grey.

Buttonhole twist in lemon.

Perlé thread, No 5, in dark green.

Aerosols of enamel car-spray paint in sky-blue and yellow.

Watercolour paint in pale green.

Stiff paper.

Making Up the Design

1 Following Fig 51, draw design onto tracing paper. Position drawing in centre of fabric and lightly mark in horizon. Mask out foreground with stiff paper. Using the sky-blue aerosol, spray the sky area so some areas are more densely coloured than others. Allow to dry.

2 Mask out sky and spray foreground yellow in the same way. Using watercolour, paint the small field at left of horizon in pale green with a soft-green line along the horizon. Referring to Transferring Your Design onto Fabric (Chapter 1), lightly mark out areas of embroidery except the foliage of the framing tree.

3 Free-machine embroider trees on horizon. Use zigzag stitch and small sideways movements to follow the outline of the trees, and allow areas of sky to show through. Stitch trees at left, mixing dull greens with a little bright green, and trees at right, intermixing brighter shades.

4 Stitch bushes below trees in same way as trees, using darker and duller shades than the trees.

5 Roughly following the line of the horizon, straight stitch spaced lines across far end of cornfield for about 1.5cm (½in) below horizon. Using lemon buttonhole twist as top thread (tighten bobbin tension if under thread (sewing thread No 40) pulls through), shorten the stitch on far lines and lengthen it on nearer lines.

6 Complete cornfield by working lines of free-machine zigzag stitch below straight stitching. Space stitching and increase width in same way as for straight stitching. Use No 40 sewing thread and shade colours through lemon, yellow and gold to soft orange. A strong swing combined with a slow speed will give a varied effect. Increase width of swing to make stitches longer towards foreground. Make sure background fabric shows through in places.

7 Work grasses in foreground in same way as cornfield, shading from lighter green to dark green at the bottom of picture. Overlap stitches over edge of cornfield and intermix colours densely to cover background completely. Stitch plant in left foreground in dark-green satin stitch.

8 With a pencil, mark in areas of framing-tree foliage on wrong side of work. Wind perlé thread on bobbin by hand and loosen tension so thread pulls through smoothly. Using sewing thread on the top of the machine and working from the wrong side, stitch foliage using a circular movement. Stitch some areas densely and allow fabric to show through in others.

9 Satin stitch poppies in red sewing thread. Add black satin-stitched eyes at centre of larger poppies. Satin stitch birds in grey.

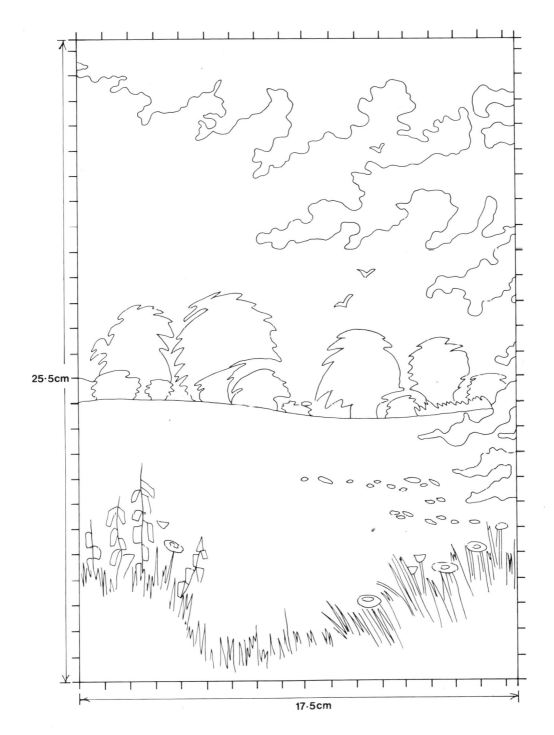

25·5cm

17·5cm

Fig 51 Diagram of English Cornfield

BOBBIE ATKINSON

Kielder Viaduct

A fairly small embroidery, worked on painted fabric which provides a coloured background for areas of delicate stitchery in the trees and grasses. In contrast, the bridge is closely couched to depict the stonework. (Colour photograph opposite.)

Materials

Ribbed silk fabric – 40cm (15¾in) square.

Stranded cotton in two shades of blue for the sky, shades of navy, dark and mid-blue for the water, shades of light, mid- and dark green, beige, camel, cream and black, plus small amounts of gold, tan and ochre.

Machine embroidery thread in tan (tan stranded cotton could be substituted).

Set of watercolours.

Embroidery ring – 30cm (11¾in) in diameter.

Making Up the Design

1 Following Fig 52, and referring to Transferring Your Design onto Fabric (Chapter 1), mark out the design centrally on the fabric and tape all edges down to a board. Allowing adjacent colours to dry so they do not run, paint the sky pale blue and the water a fairly dark mid-blue. Paint the greenery behind the viaduct a blue-green and the left bank a brighter, lighter green.

2 Insert work centrally in embroidery ring. Divide thread and use a single strand throughout unless instructions state otherwise. For stitch instructions, see Chapter 3. Work the sky in mid-blue at the top progressing down into paler blue. Stitch horizontally, as in a stem stitch, taking a long stitch on the right side and a tiny one on the wrong side. Stitch rows fairly closely together.

3 Stitch water in the same way as sky but not so closely, intermixing darker blues and navy in the darker areas and bringing in light and brighter blues near the foreground and left bank.

4 Work bridge in horizontal rows of couching, intermixing camel and cream. Couch two strands together, using a single strand of cream for the holding stitches. Work rows fairly closely to cover the area.

5 Using a darker camel shade, stitch small straight stitches at random amongst the couching. Also introduce a few tan stitches on the three supports at the right-hand side.

6 Using camel thread, outline the castellations and stitch the crosses in straight stitch. Also

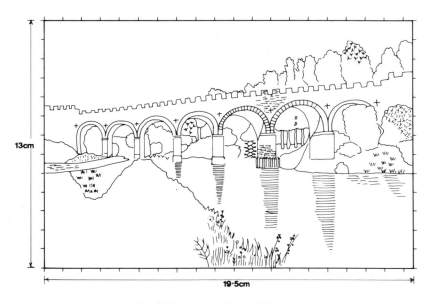

Fig 52 Diagram of Kielder Viaduct

stitch lines across the top of supports. Using cream thread, satin stitch across the base of supports and blanket stitch around the arches over the couched thread.

7 Work bushes and trees above and behind viaduct in single fly stitches. Twist a single strand of each of two different shades of green together and vary shades from bush to bush.

8 Mixing shades in the same way, work bushes at the right in front of viaduct in small, spaced seed stitches. In front of the bushes, stitch spaced clumps of small straight stitches in light green, intermixing a few beige and ochre ones along the edge of water.

9 Satin stitch shadows under the arches in black, and the area of shadow on the ground in dark green. Stitch tree-trunks in ochre satin stitch, the area below trunks in tan long-and-short stitches, and between trunks in dark-green fly stitches.

10 Stitch vertical rows of open Cretan stitch in pale-green area under third arch from right. Fill in any remaining areas behind arches in shades of green, using single fly stitches for bushes and seed stitch for grassy areas.

11 Stitch path in beige and ochre horizontal long-and-short stitch. Add grass in tan and green straight stitches behind path and a seed-stitched bush at the left in brighter shades of green.

12 For reflections of viaduct in water, use tan machine embroidery thread or split a single strand of tan stranded cotton in two and use just half. Straight stitch the reflection quite densely near base of arches, gradually increasing the space between stitches as you work downwards. Add a few green reflections near right far bank.

13 Work a small area of straight-stitched grass clumps in pale green, bright green and ochre, just below path.

14 For grassy area in foreground, use mixed bright and dull medium shades of green. Mixing shades, work random straight stitches over the areas of grass; space some densely, some sparsely and overlap some over the water's edge.

15 Using tan, beige and ochre and splitting some threads in two for extra-fine threads, work more straight stitches among the grasses; work some as clumps, some branching out like bracken and add tiny French knots to others.

Gathering Coal on Blooming Heather Shores

The embroidery, worked almost entirely in split stitch, depicts a childhood memory of days spent gathering coal on the seashore. Virtually all you need as materials are old unravelled knitting yarn and a piece of sheet for the background. (Colour photograph page 58.)

Materials

Coarsely woven cotton – 55 × 65cm (21⅝ × 25⅝in).

Oddments of knitting yarn, about 3-ply, in shades of pale blue, mid-blues, violet, sea green, sandy colours, browns and greys, plus small amounts of navy, tan, cerise, maroon, pale pink, pale, mid- and dark greens and white.

Black thread, small amount.

Grey watercolour paint.

Embroidery frame – 50 × 60cm (19⅝ × 23⅝in).

Making Up the Design

1 Following Fig 53 and referring to Transferring Your Design onto Fabric (Chapter 1), mark out the design centrally on the fabric and attach fabric to the embroidery frame. For stitch instructions, see Chapter 3. Working horizontally, stitch sky in rows of pale blue split stitch. Cover the area densely so the background does not show through.

2 Stitch mountains in same way, intermixing blue and violet yarns. Stitch the nearest mountain first, following the contour of the shape and defining the edge in darker blue. Then fill in the mountains behind in the same way.

3 Split stitch the sea, working horizontally in sea green. Then add small, random, horizontal straight stitches in mid- and dark green to give depth. Finally, stitch white highlights with small straight stitches placed at different angles.

4 Split stitch the beach horizontally in sandy shades from the shoreline to the bottom of the picture. Intermix slightly darker shades for about 1cm (⅜in) below the shoreline. Then intermix areas of different shades over the rest of the area. Leave spaces where there are solid shapes to be filled in later.

5 Using grey yarn, work small straight stitches placed at different angles over the foreground up to the top of the darker strip. Work darker strip by adding more stitches in navy and brown.

6 Work the dark areas of coal on the beach in black thread, using split stitch for the larger areas and straight stitches for the smaller pieces.

7 Stitch around the edge of waterpools in mid-brown split stitch. Fill in the centres with pale-blue split stitch. Work mid-brown split stitches randomly over the far beach area.

8 Work figures by filling in solid areas in vertical split stitch and outlining in back stitch where required. Work distant figures in dark green, the horse in tan and brown, and the cart in mid-grey with a dark-grey shaft and wheel.

9 Work figure to the right in a cerise coat with the sleeves outlined in maroon. Stitch hands and face in pale pink. Outline the face and stitch features in black thread. Stitch hair in grey, buckets in mixed greys and boots in dark grey.

10 Work figure to the left in same way. Stitch girl's coat in maroon with sleeves outlined in dark grey, the headscarf cerise, boots dark grey, and basket pale grey with a dark-grey handle. Stitch boy with a dark-grey cap, pale-grey jacket outlined in dark grey, dark-grey trousers and boots, and the spade light brown outlined in dark green.

11 Work the dog and other buckets in mid-brown split stitch outlined in dark-brown back stitch. Split stitch the large log and tree stump in mid-browns, outlined in dark-brown back stitch. Add random dark-brown and dull-green straight stitches to the log.

12 Stitch scattered branches in mid-brown back stitch with a line of dark-brown back stitch along the undersides. Stitch spade in grey split stitch with a dark-brown handle.

13 Split stitch the figure on the log in sea greens with darker green in the shaded area. Stitch hands in pink and scarf in cerise.

14 Outline top of cart, wheel and nearest handle in pale-green back stitch. Outline underside of cart, handle and outside of wheel in navy back

stitch. Fill in the rest of cart in dull-green split stitch. Add a few sand-coloured straight stitches to top of near edge, at top of handle and at centre of wheel.

15 Using grey watercolour paint, paint grey cloudy areas on the sky. Split stitch seagulls in white and grey. Straight stitch the more distant birds in black thread.

Fig 53 Diagram of Gathering Coal on Blooming Heather Shores

Gathering Coal on Blooming Heather Shores

SHEENA SHAW

Highland Spring

Worked against a smooth, blue satin-stitched sky, the trees stand out starkly in both their colour and texture of knobbly French knots. The play of light and dark is repeated in the water's reflection, illustrated simply and effectively in straight stitches. (Colour photograph below.)

Materials

Fine even-weave cotton backing fabric – 40cm (15¾in) square.

Stranded cotton in three shades of pale turquoise, cream, grey, ecru, two shades of dark green, coffee, dark brown, tan and black, plus extra shades of dull turquoise and grey and navy for the water.

Embroidery ring – 30cm (11¾in) in diameter.

Making Up the Design

1 Following Fig 54 and referring to Transferring Your Design onto Fabric (Chapter 1), mark out the design centrally on the backing fabric and insert in embroidery ring. For stitch instructions, see Chapter 3. Divide stranded cotton and using a single strand, stitch the sky in long vertical satin stitches. Use the darker shades of pale turquoise at the left and the medium shade at the right of the trees.

2 Work the clouds in cream with some segments in the palest turquoise. Using a single strand, satin stitch the clouds in segments, varying the angle of stitching in each segment.

3 Fill in trunks and branches of tall trees and dark areas below trees in small, vertical,

overlapping straight stitches, using two strands of dark-brown thread. Work smaller branches in stem stitch. To give the appearance of foliage, fill in the areas indicated on the diagram with closely-packed French knots.

4 Working from skyline downwards, satin stitch grey areas behind trees using a single strand of thread. Using two strands of thread, work bands of green and ecru satin stitch between the grey and dark-brown stitching.

5 Fill in the area below ecru stitching and along the headland in tan French knots (two strands). Work areas between the dark-brown stitching on left shoreline with random straight stitches and French knots in coffee-coloured thread (two strands).

6 Stitch distant mountain on right in grey satin stitch (one strand). Near the peak, overwork small areas of the grey in cream satin stitch worked at different angles to the grey stitching.

7 Stitch centre mountain in ecru in the same way as the first mountain, but varying the angle of the stitching. Overwork peak of this mountain with small areas of cream and grey.

8 Vary the angle of the stitching again for the two mountains on the left. Work in satin stitch using ecru thread and introducing areas of cream near the peaks.

9 Work small hill to the right of tall trees in small blocks of alternating vertical and horizontal satin stitch. Use a dull green and a single strand of thread.

10 Using two strands of thread, work individual trees between mountains and shoreline in graduated satin stitch. Work distant trees in dark green, introducing more trees in mixed green and coffee and some in plain coffee near the shoreline. Pack trees densely together.

11 Work side of boat in three bands of vertical satin stitch using two strands of black thread.

12 Outline top of boat with one row of white stem stitch (two strands) and one row of coffee (one strand). Stitch seat half in white and half in coffee, using satin stitch. Satin stitch white rectangle and fill in the rest of the interior in black satin stitch and stem stitch (two strands).

13 Work water in straight overlapping stitches, using two strands of thread. Work a strip along far shoreline in dull mid-turquoise, then a strip across from the headland in pale turquoise.

14 Work water to the right in shades of turquoise, adding in a few dark-navy stitches and more grey towards the bottom of the picture.

15 Work reflections of the tree-trunks in navy with grey stitches between trunks and other dark areas in navy and grey. Bring in more dark turquoise with grey and a little navy towards the right of the picture. Stitch anchor line of boat in black stem stitch and buoy in satin stitch (two strands).

Fig 54 Diagram of Highland Spring

ERICA WOODMAN

Loch Torridon at Dusk

This highly stylised sunset view uses simple stitch-work and appliqué to great effect. The shimmering water is symbolised brilliantly by lurex fabric shaded with stranded cotton satin stitch. (Colour photograph page 63.)

Materials

Deep-turquoise base fabric – 50cm (19⅝in) square.

Silver lurex fabric – 30 × 50cm (11¾ × 19⅝in).

Oddments of various fabrics: pale bluey-grey synthetic suede (A); pale-blue shantung (B); mid-blue shantung (C); dark-grey poplin (D); black synthetic suede (E).

Stranded cotton in various tones of grey, blue, turquoise, green and brown, plus cream, white and black.

Embroidery frame – 46cm (18¼in) square.

Making Up the Design

1 Following Fig 55 and referring to Transferring Your Design onto Fabric (Chapter 1), mark out the design on the centre of the base fabric. Tack lurex over lower half of design, just up to central strip above hills and insert in frame. For stitch instructions, see Chapter 3. Blanket stitch top edge of lurex in place.

2 Following the diagram, appliqué areas of sky in fabrics indicated, using blanket stitch to secure them to the backing fabric.

3 Cut out the three hills in black suede and stitch in place in the same way.

4 Begin to work the water reflections by using three strands of stranded cotton together. Using stem stitch and various shades of grey, work short-and-long stitches close to base edge of hills, making the stitches denser within the cove areas and at the lower two corners of the work. Work grey thread in the same way at the top edge of the meeting of the two top hills. Changing to cream thread and three strands, work a band of stem stitch in various lengths along the top edge of the lurex fabric, taking the stitches over to the right between the hills. Work a thick line of cream stitching within the band of base fabric just above the lurex, with a thinner one just below this. Add highlights of yellow and white stitching to the cove at the base of the hill on the far left.

5 Starting at the base of the appliquéd sections of the sky, work stem stitch in a variety of turquoise and grey shades, using two strands together and working the stitches more densely towards the right-hand side. Leave the suede sky area fairly free from embroidery, working a few long stitches centrally across it. Using satin stitch and a pale turquoise thread, add puffs of cloud to the bottom and top areas of the blue-suede area and up into the top left-hand corner of the work.

6 Working with three strands of dark-grey thread, work tightly packed stem stitch on the top of the dark-grey poplin hill.

7 To add density and texture to the hills, change to one thread of green and one of brown worked together, and work very small stem stitches in random patches over the large hill in the foreground and the hill on the left-hand side.

8 Add a few small trees to the top edge of the foreground hill, using one strand of black thread and small straight stitches.

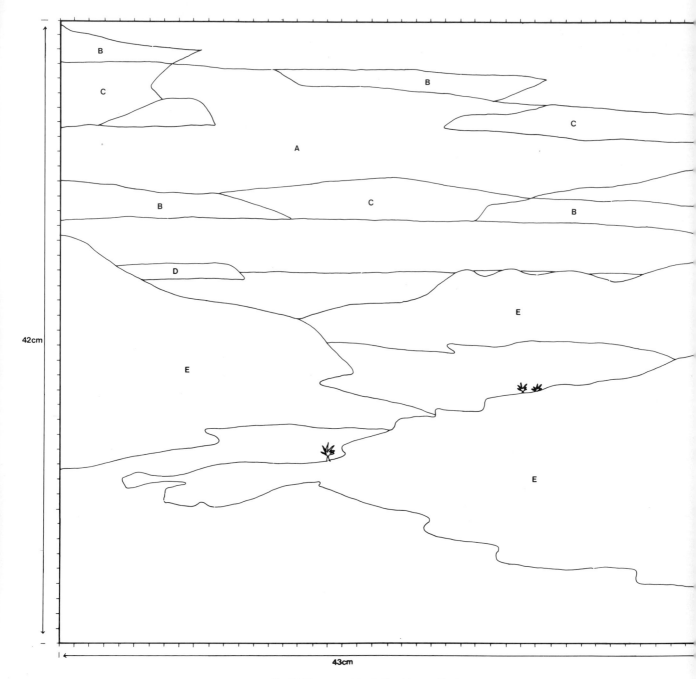

Fig 55 Diagram of Loch Torridon at Dusk

Loch Torridon at Dusk

Sandy Shore

NB Unfortunately, we cannot trace a name for this piece – we apologise to its anonymous creator, and hope she will contact us at Living Magazine.

This design uses anything and everything imaginable to create a shore that would delight any beachcomber – there's string, sandpaper, buttons, beads, sequins, cellophane and the inevitable sea shells! A combination of machine and hand work has been used to give a sculptural feel. (Colour photograph page 11.)

Materials

Beige base fabric – 50 × 80cm (19⅝ × 31½in).
Large sheets of sandpaper.
Oddments of the following fabrics: pale-blue lining; white and pale-blue net; rust lining; synthetic brown sheepskin; brown and cream check brushed cotton; green lining; cream and brown quilted fabric; pale-turquoise lining.
Oddments of trimmings including: white ribbon; white lace; gold braid; silver and white striped ribbon.
Selection of matt and shiny threads from tapestry wool to embroidery silks in colours that match and tone with the fabric oddments.
Buttons, beads, sequins, curtain rings and shells in all shapes, colours and sizes.
Pearly plastic mesh (used for fruit and vegetable bags).
Cling-film cellophane.
Clear plastic (used for shirt boxes and packaging).
Embroidery ring – 20cm (7⅞in) diameter.

Making Up the Design

1 Following Fig 56 and referring to Transferring Your Design onto Fabric (Chapter 1), draw the areas of the design onto the base fabric. Cut out the sea shape in pale-turquoise lining and tack in position. Place the work in the embroidery ring and set the machine to a medium-width open zigzag stitch. Using various shades of turquoise sewing thread, work random lines of stitching over the entire lining area, carrying the stitching slightly over onto the base fabric. As you machine, incorporate small pieces of the clear plastic into the work to give the water a reflective feel. Remove work from ring.

2 Cut out cloud shapes from pale-blue lining and blue and white net. Position them on the work, leaving an area of base fabric showing. Place a piece of blue net over entire sky area and tack down around all edges. Scrunch up small lengths of lace and ribbon and hand sew to areas of the sky to represent puffs of cloud. For stitch instructions, see Chapter 3. Using white sewing thread and fly stitch, work rows of stitching around the ribbon areas, following the contour of the sky. Sew pearly sequins and beads around the ribbon as highlights. Create wispy tails of cloud using lengths of white wool couched to the background fabric.

3 The hill area is made up of lengths of the various brown fabrics scrunched up and attached to the base fabric using an occasional hand stitch to hold the fabric in position. More texture is added to this area with lengths of a variety of yarns and braids couched over the fabric. Add feather stitches worked in sewing threads to the flatter areas of fabric. The top and base of the hill are highlighted with beads, sequins and buttons in gold, green and orange.

4 Sandpaper is used for the beach. Tear it into irregular shapes to fit the area indicated on the diagram. With the machine set on an open, medium-width zigzag stitch and using beige sewing thread, work some lines of stitching over the sandpaper to give the appearance of lines in the sand. Position the paper on the design, overlapping torn edges and securing in place with a few hand stitches.

5 Where the edge of the hill meets the sand and sea, add interest with lengths of scrunched-up braid, tapestry wool and blue net.

6 The water's edge is symbolised by wrinkled pieces of cling film following the contour of the beach and held down with a few single hand stitches. Emphasise this edge with lengths of silver ribbon couched in place.

7 Complete the design with an array of articles scattered over the sand. Cluster them towards the front of the design and attach with single hand stitches. Couch a piece of plastic mesh around this area. Add clusters of sequins to the sea area to give the appearance of the crests of waves.

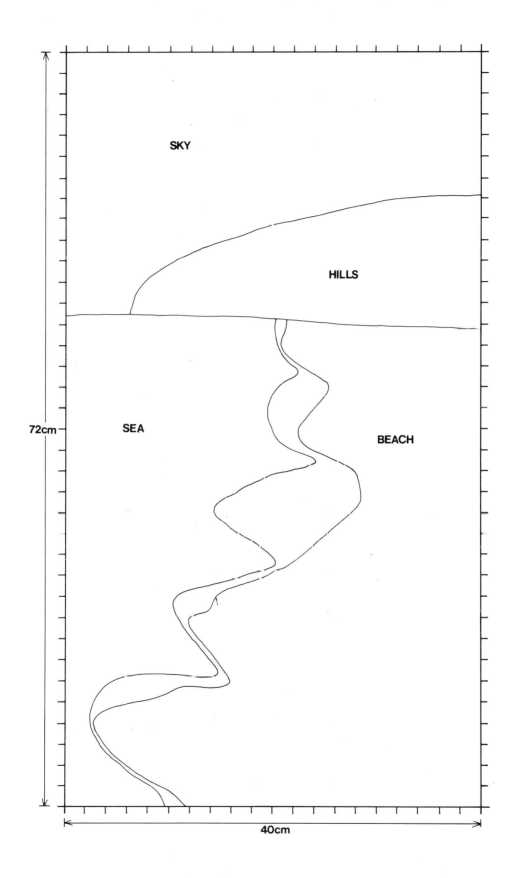

Fig 56 Diagram of Sandy Shore (each square represents 2cm)

JOAN STEVENSON

Light in the Western Sky

This stylised view of a sunset over Glenvig Bay is created by appliqué and fabric paint. The reflections are highlighted by simple straight stitches. (Colour photograph below).

Materials

Pink cotton poplin – 40 × 50cm (15¾ × 19⅝in).
Oddments of pale-green cotton poplin.
Sewing threads in shades of pale green, navy and orange.
Fabric paints.
Embroidery frame – 36cm (14¼in) square.

Making Up the Design

1 Following Fig 57, draw design onto tracing paper. Lightly mark out the design centrally on the pink poplin, referring to Transferring Your Design onto Fabric (Chapter 1). The work is made up of different sections of green fabric appliquéd onto the pink background. Once each section is appliquéd, it is painted before subsequent sections are appliquéd over it. Trace each piece indicated by a letter from the initial drawing and cut out in fabric, leaving a small turning (3–4mm – ⅛–¼in) along all edges. These turnings should be pressed to the wrong side and the section invisibly slipstitched in place. For stitch instructions, see Chapter 3.

2 Place the main fabric in embroidery frame and appliqué sections A, B, C, D, E, F and G in place.

3 Mix fabric paints to give a selection of different peach tones. With the work out of frame, paint pale-peach tones from below section A to above section D, darkening the peach colour around section C. Apply pale-peach paint to fabric between H and E, painting a darker peach line

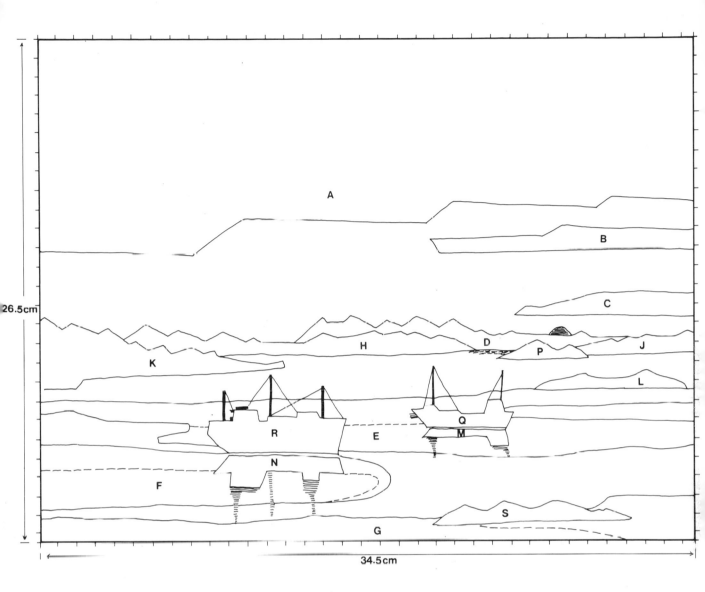

Fig 57 Diagram of Light in the Western Sky

centrally above the E area and using the same colour between right-hand sections of E. Paint section between E and G, keeping pale peach around the curve created by F and giving this area a darker central band.

4 Mix paints to give various tones of turquoise green, from light to very dark sea-green. Paint in areas B and C with pale turquoise. Use the same colour to paint in the top half of section E, around the top edge of section F and the right-hand corner of section G. Use a shade darker to cover section D.

5 Set work back into frame (always remove when paint is to be applied) and appliqué section H. Paint this section a still darker turquoise.

6 Appliqué the sections J, K and L. Darken turquoise paint a little more and paint in these areas. Using the same colour, paint a thin line across top edge of section F and dashes of colour following the peach reflection to the right of this section.

7 Appliqué sections P, Q, R and S. Paint these areas and the boat reflections N and M.

8 Using a single strand of orange thread, satin stitch sun to the top right-hand edge of section D. Straight stitch the sun's reflection across the lower edge of section D between H and P and stitch fine lines above, between and below right-hand sections of E. Satin stitch lamp on mast of left-hand boat in orange thread.

9 Using a single strand of navy thread, satin stitch masts, using long single stitches for the rigging. Add thread highlights to the dashes of paint above section G and below and to the right of section S. Use spaced-out satin stitches of various lengths below N and M to give the reflection of the boats more reality.

Fig 58 Diagram of Morris Dancing

57·5cm

42cm

JOAN EDWARDS

Morris Dancing

This is a lively piece of work which uses a wide variety of interesting fabrics to depict a typically English country scene. A large proportion of the design is constructed using simple stuck-down appliqué, with stitches to accentuate parts of the design. (Colour photograph page 70.)

Materials

Pale creamy-blue base fabric – 50 × 70cm (19⅝ × 27½in).

Grey flannel suiting – 25 × 70cm (9⅞ × 27½in) (A).

Oddments of the following fabrics: rust corduroy (B); grey-striped flannel (C); brown and cream flecked flannel (D); brown-striped flannel (E); cream silk (F); white jersey (G); fancy brown tweed (H); sage-green flannel (I); black gabardine (J); black felt (K); white felt (L); black synthetic leather (M); flesh-coloured jersey (N); white tights fabric (O); striped black and white fabric (P).

Green, brown and black tapestry wool.

Oddments of ribbon in green, yellow, maroon, beige and black.

Black and white embroidery cotton.

Black and white paper.

Card.

Small yellow beads.

Adhesive.

Felt-tip pens.

Cocktail sticks.

Making Up the Design

1 Following Fig 58, trace the background section of the design onto tracing paper. Cut out the pieces of the design in the fabric indicated and stick them down to the base fabric. Start with the row of houses at the back of the work. Stick down the main sections, followed by their roofs. Cut out the window frames in white card then place on a rectangle of black card cut to the same size. Stick lines of brown tapestry wool along the sides of the two brown houses to give the effect of beams. Stick lines of black wool in the same way on the front of the white building on the left-hand side.

2 Couch brown tapestry wool in position to the right- and left-hand side of the sky in the position shown on the diagram. Cut 2cm (¾in) wide strips of sage-green flannel and fray the two long sides. Cut into smaller pieces and stick over thread branches on trees on right-hand side. Add extra texture by working knots around the branches in green tapestry wool, then cutting the threads to leave 2–3cm (¾–1⅛in) thread-ends. Work the leaves on the tree to the left side of the work in the same way, using knots of threads left with long ends.

3 Stick the foreground grey-flannel suiting in place. Cut out the various sections of the policeman and the horse and stick in position.

Fig 59 Diagram for morris men

You may find it easier to stick the gabardine fabric to the card first, then cut out the sections. Add a tail and mane in black embroidery cotton with a narrow strip of synthetic leather forming the reins. Sew a ring of white felt in place for the eye and two rows of white satin stitch for the teeth. Beads can be sewn to the fringe of the horse's cover and the front of the policeman's jacket.

4 Cut out the old man on the right and the man and his dog on the left in various flannel fabrics with flesh-coloured jersey for their hands and faces. Stick them down in position, painting in their features with felt-tip pens. Hair can be added with small cuts of tapestry wool.

5 The morris men are all made using the same basic technique. Following Fig 59, cut out the man in card, cutting out a separate piece for each section, ie, the body, arms, legs, face and so on. The diagram shows the morris man cut to one size but the size of the different parts of the body can be altered to give men of different heights and proportions. Each card section is covered in the fabric indicated, with the fabric taken round to the wrong side and held in place with a few stitches. Decorate each section of the body, then stick down in the chosen position. The body section should have irregular lengths of various-coloured ribbons stuck in position, and the legs green ribbon and black cotton threads tied around at the knee. Beads can be sewn to these to resemble bells. Tie lengths of black cotton around the elbows as armbands and white thread around the hats. The faces are given features with various-coloured felt-tip pens. Six complete morris men have been stuck to the design, with part of a figure stuck behind the man to the far left. For an authentic and three-dimensional look, attach lengths of cocktail sticks to their hands in the traditional cross manner. A brown tapestry-wool tuft added to the head of the morris man on the right and decorated with ribbon distinguishes this man as the fool.

6 Work green tapestry-wool tufts to the far left-hand side of the white house and around the group of morris men to the left. Work a small group of the same tufts below the roof of the house on the right and between the policeman and the horse's mane.

SARAH DODDS

A Cornish Medley

This sampler, worked mainly in cross stitch, has favourite images of Cornwall worked within a formal floral border. Worked clockwise the scenes depict: Longships Lighthouse, the sword Excalibur, a puffin, Botallack tin mine, St Pirran's Cross, Boscastle harbour, the Egyptian House in Penzance, a crab, Royal Albert bridge over the Tamar, and a mermaid. (Colour photograph page 18.)

Materials

Even-weave linen, 14 threads over 2.5cm (1in) – 47cm (18½in) square.
Stranded threads in rose pink, pale grey, dark blue, dark green, lime green, pale green, black, white and cream, plus shades of grey, soft blues, bright blues, soft yellows, greens, peaches and pinks, tans and beige, violet and several shades of lilac, plus small amounts of red and emerald.
Squared graph paper.
Coloured crayons.
Embroidery frame – 40cm (15¾in) square.

Making Up the Design

1 Following the stitch plan and allowing one square per stitch, mark out centrally on graph paper the words, the mermaid, the cross and the portions of side borders as given. Also mark in the portions of central borders above and below the quotation given at either side of stitch plan.

Fig 60 Stitch plan for A Cornish Medley

2 Repeating the stitch plan given, draw in the rest of the central borders above and below the words. Referring to Fig 61 and repeating stitch plan given, draw in the remainder of floral side borders.

3 A portion of the top and bottom floral border is given below the words on the stitch plan. The squares marked by circles show how the side borders will join in at the corners. Simply turn the plan upside down for top corners. Repeating stitch plan draw in borders across top and bottom.

4 Scale up the design diagram to match the size of the stitch plan and lightly transfer sections of the design to the stitch plan on graph paper (each square on the stitch plan represents one stitch). If you are fairly experienced, work straight onto the fabric following the stitch plan; the less experienced will find it simpler to make a complete stitch plan at this point. Refer to Fig 61 and the photograph (page 18), and colour each section in the shade in which it will be stitched. For stitch instructions, see Chapter 3.

5 Divide thread and use three strands together throughout. Stitch cross stitches over a single thread unless instructions say otherwise. Work words centrally in rose pink. Work border above words in pale grey and border below in dark blue.

6 Cross and mermaid: stitch cross at right of words in tan with darker tan details. Stitch mermaid's body in peach, hair yellow, flares

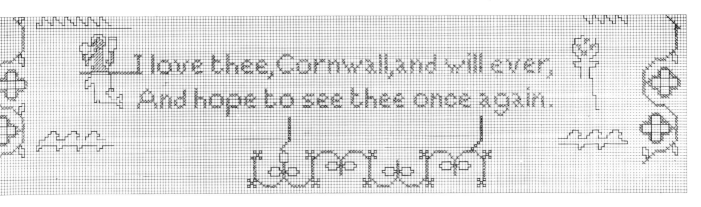

lilac, and tail alternate dark-green and lime-green stitches with lime-green fins. Stitch eyes blue and mouth red.

7 Border: stitch border outline in dark green. On side borders, stitch pale-green leaves and outline the flowers in rose pink. Stitch squares of satin stitch within the flowers with a contrasting square at the centre. Vary colours from flower to flower.

8 Stitch leaves at top and bottom of borders, shown by squares on stitch plan, in lime green. Stitch flowers, varying colours from group to group.

9 Lighthouse: stitch lighthouse white with light-grey windows. Use mixed soft yellows for light rays. Stitch over the light with criss-crossed straight stitches in one strand of black thread. Satin stitch areas of sky surrounding lighthouse

Fig 61 Design diagram of A Cornish Medley

in greys and soft blues. Stitch rocks tan with blue, pale-green and white water at the base of lighthouse.

10 Excalibur: stitch sword dark green with a bright-pink handguard, and pink and emerald decoration. Stitch the hand and arm in peach and the sleeve in pale green. Stitch water in light and dark shades of soft blue.

11 Puffin: stitch puffin black with a small grey area on its back and a white underbody. Stitch leg in tan, head in pale grey and beak in yellow and red. Stitch over the ends of wings and tail in grey and black satin stitch.

12 Tin mine: outline the tin mine, windows and entrance in grey. Stitch rocks to left and solid areas of chimney in grey. Stitch lines above windows and chimney stack in tan, and windows and entrance in black. Stitch blocks of four grey stitches on mine to represent bricks and single alternate grey stitches in chimney. Stitch sky in peach and pinks, sea in blues, and ground in greens and tans with a grey path. Stitch a band of mixed grey, tan and beige across the foreground.

13 Harbour: stitch boats in blues and white with red, yellow, cream and tan highlights. Stitch water in blocks of random satin stitch in soft greyish blues with white at the shoreline. Stitch beach in beige and harbour walls in greys.

14 Egyptian House: stitch the main background of house in violet with lilac areas around windows and doors. Outline windows in white with white tracery and fill in with pale grey. Work chequerboard borders in blue and cream, with yellow and dark lilac above middle side windows. Stitch horizontal lines above window and pediment in tan, underlined with lilac at top of house and dark lilac on ground-floor windows. Stitch base edge of house in dark lilac with alternate light- and dark-lilac stitches on the entrance. Stitch the pediments in yellow, and the statues in yellow with tan, black and blue details.

15 Bridge: stitch supports and archway in shades of tan. Stitch bridge struts in vertical rows of blue cross stitch, with long single-strand stitches between the top of each strut and the base of the next one. Outline top and bottom of struts in dull blue. Stitch the rest of bridge and entrance in grey. Stitch water in bright and dull blues. Stitch railway timbers black and the lines in grey.

16 Crab: stitch the lines on crab and the legs in dark peach. Stitch pincers and eyes in black. Stitch the rest of the crab symmetrically in soft shades of tan, peach and yellow.

Highland Reflections

The background of this Highland landscape is worked in an impressionistic way – long stem and straight stitches of different colours are intermixed to look like brush strokes. The foreground is sharply in focus, with flowers and foliage clearly defined in more traditional stitchery. (Colour photograph opposite.)

Materials

Tan-coloured hessian – 40cm (15¾in) square.
Stranded cotton in several shades of grey, pale blue, light and dark blue, green and turquoise, plus small amounts of lilac, cream, white, beige, camel, lemon, soft pink, bright pink and various browns.

Fine tapestry wool in shades of dull turquoise, grey, soft blue and dark to medium greens, plus small amounts of brown, cream, beige, camel and dull pink.
Embroidery ring – 30cm (11¾in) in diameter.

Making Up the Design

1 Following Fig 62 and referring to Transferring Your Design onto Fabric (Chapter 1), mark out design on the centre of the fabric and insert fabric in the embroidery ring. With this particular design, it is a good idea to refer to the colour photograph throughout making up, to see how the shades of colour are intermixed. For stitch instructions, see Chapter 3.

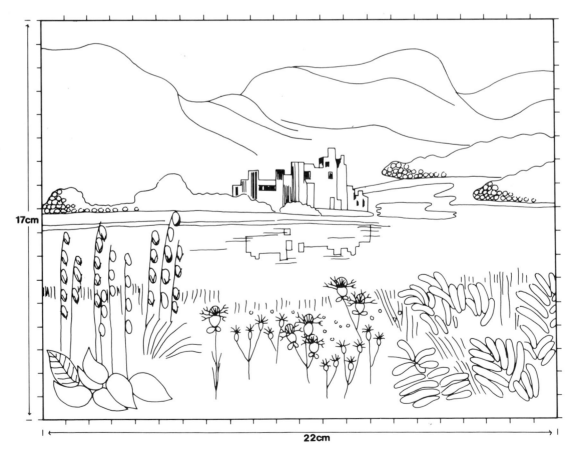

17cm

22cm

Fig 62 Diagram of Highland Reflections

2 Begin with the central mountain, using tapestry wool in shades of dull turquoise, greys and soft blues. Following the contour of the mountain, stitch in long stem stitches, intermixing the colours. Use grey predominantly at the top, switching to a dull turquoise lower down. Outline the peaks in grey stranded cotton (six strands) using stem stitch.

3 Fill in the distant mountains on the right in the same way, using grey at the top and shading down into greens and browns.

4 Begin stitching mountains on the left, starting with the more distant one. Use blue, grey, green and brown tapestry wool, mixing in stranded cotton (two or three strands) in all shades of green. Increase the amount of green stranded cotton, stitching towards the lower land. Stitch lower land at centre of picture in shades of mid-green stranded cotton (two strands).

5 Stitch sky in the same way, using stranded cotton (two strands) in shades of grey, turquoise and pale blue, plus a little white and lilac. Stitch crosswise, curving the lines of stitching down a little at each end.

6 Stitch castle in vertical stem stitch, with random straight stitches over the smaller areas. Use tapestry wool, intermixing camel, beige and cream with dark brown for shadows and highlights in cream stranded cotton (two strands).

7 Work shadowed part of castle in same way, intermixing mid-browns with dark blues and using dark brown for the darker, shadowed areas.

8 Using similar colours as for castle but in stranded cotton (two strands) stitch reflection in water in straight stitches spaced apart so that the background fabric shows through.

9 Stem stitch horizontally the strip of land below

castle and around the bay on the right in shades of green stranded cotton (two strands). Fill in wooded areas to left of castle and around the bay with French knots worked in tapestry wool. Use darker greens at the base and lighter green above.

10 Work water in horizontal stem stitch, allowing background fabric to show through in places. Use stranded cotton (two strands) in shades of dark and light blue, dull and bright turquoise, dark and light greys and pale green, with a little lemon for highlights.

11 Stitch foreground with long straight stitches in clumps of all shades of green stranded cotton (two strands). Overlap some stitches over the edge of the water and allow background to show through in places.

12 Stitch stems of tall flowers in stem stitch, using mid-green tapestry wool. Work detached chain-stitch flowers in dull-pink tapestry wool. Add straight-stitched, bright-pink highlights to flowers in stranded cotton (two strands).

13 Work flat leaves below flowers in mid- and dark-green tapestry wool using Roumanian stitch. Stem stitch the curved grasses to right of flowers in shades of green tapestry wool.

14 Work pink thistles in stranded cotton (two strands). Straight stitch dark-green stems with two detached chain stitches at the top. Stitch bulb of thistle with two dark-brown detached chain stitches side by side and partly over-lapping. Satin stitch flower-centres in dark and pale pink, then add single pale-pink fly stitches on long stalks radiating from centre.

15 Work lemon flowers in stranded cotton. Straight stitch stalks in green (two strands). Work single, detached chain stitches at top of stalks in dark green (two strands). Straight stitch the flowers in lemon (three strands).

16 Stitch foliage at right in light, medium and dark shades of green stranded cotton (three strands) using Pekinese stitch. Add a few French knots in white stranded cotton (two strands) among the flowers in the centre.

IRENE MACWILLIAM

Palm House

A combination of appliquéd fabric, ordinary machine embroidery and free-machine embroidery techniques are used in this large and intricate design. Fine organdie mounted on interfacing is used for the palm house; behind this are plant shapes which stand out clearly when the embroidery is held against the light. (Colour photograph page 79.)

Materials
White cotton fabric – 46 × 50cm (18⅛ × 19⅝in).
White organdie – 30 × 45cm (11¾ × 17¾in).
White interfacing, very lightweight iron-on – 30 × 45cm (11¾ × 17¾in).
Light brown-grey fabric – 5 × 45cm (2 × 17¾in).
Light-green fabric – 10 × 45cm (4 × 17¾in).
Small pieces of mid- and dark-green fabric, floral fabrics and white cotton.
Rayon machine-embroidery thread in white, pale grey and light blue.
Sewing or machine-embroidery threads in shades of bright, light, mid- and dark green and brown.
Buttonhole twist in dark green.
Machine-embroidery shaded thread in cream-brown and peach-orange.
Fabric paint in pale blue, grey, brown and dull green.
Modeller's airbrush.
Embroidery ring – 20cm (7⅞in) in diameter.

Making Up the Design
1 Following Fig 63, draw out the design on tracing paper. This tracing should be laid over the embroidery as you work to check the correct positioning of different parts of the design. Mark out the design area to be worked centrally on white background fabric. Using modeller's airbrush and fabric paint, paint sky area in softly shaded blue. Allow to dry.
2 Cut out plant shapes (given as dotted lines on diagram) for within palm house in mixed green and floral fabrics. Tack pieces in place.
3 Cut out dense part of large bush on left in dark-green fabric. Tack in place. Paint soft-brown branches on fabric and bush area above fabric.
4 Insert fabric in embroidery ring when working

areas of free-machine embroidery. Free-machine embroider (see section on machine embroidery in Chapter 3) brown branches at centre of bush, then work random machine embroidery over entire bush shape in shades of mid- and dark-green sewing threads.
5 Paint in rough areas of dull green on the brown-grey strip of fabric and cut out path shape, allowing a little extra fabric on each edge for underlaps. Tack in place.
6 Lightly apply interfacing to organdie. Cut out the entire palm-house shape and tack in place. Overlay strips of white cotton fabric along the band at the base of houses and the strip with three decorative panels at top of smaller house. Tack in place.
7 Using white rayon thread, machine around side and top edge of houses in medium-width satin stitch. Stitch around the top white strip and top edge of base white strip in the same way. Stitch lower edge of base strip with a wide satin stitch in white.
8 Change to pale-grey thread and a medium-width satin stitch. Stitch below white stitching at base edge and top straight edge of main house. At top of main house, stitch far struts, long, oval struts and arched struts, all marked by a double line on diagram. Also stitch the sloping end of smaller house.
9 Change to white thread (still medium-width) satin stitch. Stitch all remaining vertical struts on both houses. Stitch around skylights on smaller house and two more rows above fabric strip at top of this house with a wider row above the decorative panel to the left.
10 Using a small straight stitch and white thread, stitch two or three evenly spaced rows between each vertical white strut on both houses.
11 Stitch horizontal lines in satin stitch: about halfway down dome of main house, stitch a row of narrow white. Spaced a little way below that, stitch a row of medium-width white with a grey row below that. At base of dome and top of side walls, stitch bands of wide white, then stitch a row of narrow grey below the two on main house.

35·5cm

38·5cm

Fig 63 Diagram of Palm House

12 Work two rows of pre-set machine-embroidery stitches below the satin stitch at top of side walls on both houses. Stitch two rows, one white and one blue, across the top of both houses.

13 Paint rectangles on white strip of smaller house using grey paint. Straight stitch a few rows around rectangles in white thread, then free-machine embroider interlacing stitches over the grey rectangles.

14 Cut pale- and dark-green fabrics to shape for foreground areas. Cut mid-green fabrics to shape of remaining three bushes. Cut out deep notches around top edges of pampas-bush pieces. Tack all fabric pieces in place, under-

lapping if necessary.

15 Using zigzag stitch, free-machine embroider bush at far left with random stitching in shades of dark and mid-green, with just a little pale green.

16 Free-machine embroider pale-green area of foreground in bright and light greens, bringing in darker green on the shaded areas. Stitch in an up-and-down zigzag motion, overlapping edge of path in places and allowing fabric to show through.

17 Using buttonhole twist, free-machine embroider over darker green fabric area in angular tufts, allowing background fabric to show through. Using shaded orange thread and zigzag stitch, free-machine embroider star-like flowers over the dark-green area.

18 Free-machine embroider pampas bushes in mixed shades of green. Keep stitching fairly straight and arching out from the base of the plant. Overlap stitches over the edge of the fabric.

19 Work pampas plumes in cream and brown shaded thread with two threads through the machine needle. Use a machine tailor-tacking foot and a very short stitch length. Stitch about three rows of machine tailor tacking very close together. Iron on small pieces of interfacing to back of stitching and snip through the loops of thread on the right side of work.

LYNN FINKELSTEIN

Plymouth Hoe

This bold scene is made up of many layers of appliqué and rows of machine stitching. A three-dimensional effect is given to the clouds, cliff top and lighthouse with wadding. (Colour photograph page 82.)

Materials

Light-turquoise base fabric – 80cm (31½in) square (A).

Lilac grosgrain – 30 × 80cm (11¾ × 31½in) (B).

Green canvas – 20 × 80cm (7⅞ × 31½in) (C).

Pale-blue chiffon – 50 × 80cm (19⅝ × 31½in) (D).

Oddments of the following fabrics: dark-green towelling; sage-green synthetic suede; maroon and cream corduroy; various textured fabrics in shades of purple and lilac for the sea area; dark-green scraps for cliff top; yellow, red, white, blue, brown and tan felt. Plastic window and balcony shapes for lighthouse (these could be cut from the white felt, with cellophane behind the window).

Selection of sewing threads to match fabrics.

Fabric adhesive.

Oddments of wadding.

Embroidery ring – 20cm (7⅞in) diameter.

Making Up the Design

1 Following Fig 64, draw the design to full size on tracing paper. Trace off the cloud section and cut out in chiffon. Tack in position on base fabric, placing thin layers of wadding underneath to form puffy clouds. Place work in embroidery ring. Set machine to a medium-width, closely worked zigzag stitch (machine satin stitch) and using pale-blue thread, work stitching around entire outside edge of cloud area. Add random machine lines in white thread over the cloud area.

2 Place lilac grosgrain in position and machine top edge in position using lilac sewing thread and machine satin stitch. Work one row of green and one row of yellow satin stitch 1cm (⅜in) above this horizon line.

3 Cut out island shapes using green towelling for furthermost island and sage synthetic suede for the other two. Satin stitch in place using yellow

thread and wrinkling up the front island slightly as you machine. Add stitching detail to the front two islands, using dark-green thread and working random rows of narrow zigzag stitching.

4 The sea area is made up of different sections of purple and lilac fabric appliquéd to the lilac grosgrain background. Cut out irregular shapes in the fabric and machine in place using a medium-width machine satin stitch in various toning shades of thread.

5 Cut out green-canvas area and machine satin stitch top edge in place. Secure a layer of wadding underneath this section to give the cliff top a three-dimensional feel. Cut irregular strips of green fabric and machine satin stitch over cliff-top area using various shades of green thread. Work lines of random straight stitch over these green areas to give a highly textured look.

6 Cut out lighthouse sections in cream and maroon corduroy, adding a 5mm (¼in) seam allowance where the sections meet. Seam the lighthouse sections together and place in position on work. Lightly pad shape, then appliqué down to base fabric, using machine satin stitch and changing thread colour as you work around the outside edge of the lighthouse.

7 Cut out a piece of blue chiffon the size of the window and stitch in place with the window secured in position over this area. Hand-stitch the balcony in place.

8 Cut out man in felt, giving him a white face and hands. Stick in position.

9 Cut out kite sections in red and yellow felt with kite bows in red felt. Stick the main kite section in position with a curved length of cotton thread for the tail. Stitch bows of felt along this length. Attach a length of the same thread to the middle of the main kite section and take it down to the man's hand, where it should be cut off and stuck in position.

10 Cut out boat shapes using brown and tan felt for the hulls and white felt for the sails. Stick in position along foreground of sea area.

73cm

72cm

Fig 64 Diagram of Plymouth Hoe (each square represents 2cm)

Plymouth Hoe, see page 80

Rain Clouds over the Beacons,
see page 84

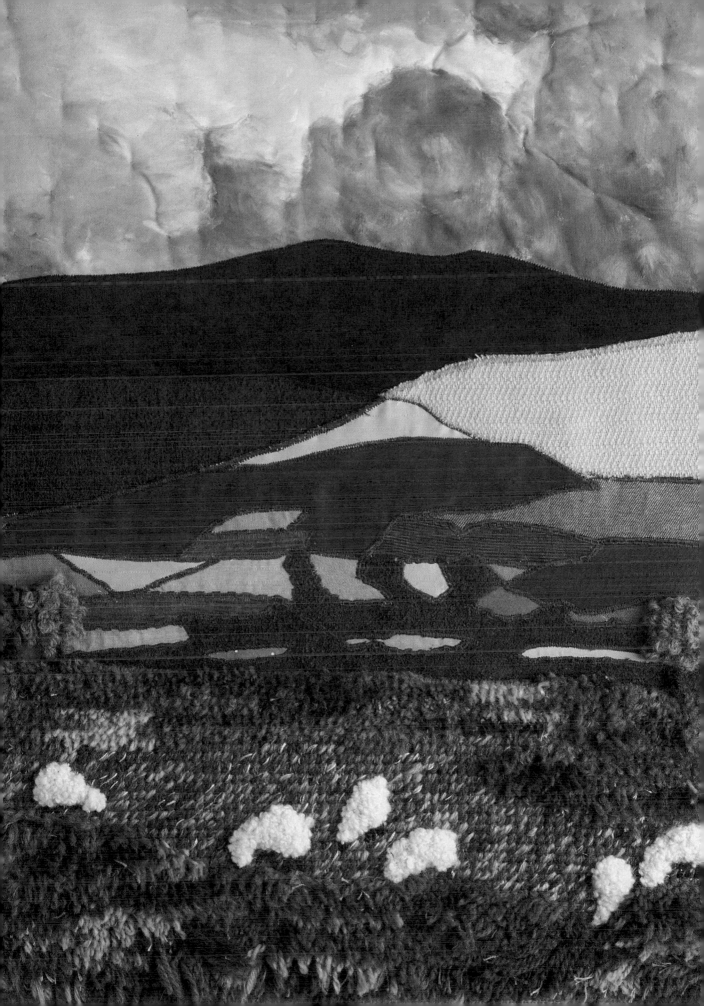

JANET PHILLIPS

Rain Clouds over the Beacons

This picture is made up of appliquéd sections of textured fabrics – the foreground being a section of rugwork! Some sections of the work, such as the sheep, are highly padded. (Colour photograph page 83.)

Materials

Natural hessian – 60 × 90cm (23⅝ × 35½in).

Oddments of the following fabrics: grey poplin (A); navy velveteen (B); lightweight beige tweed (C); pale-green cotton poplin (D); leaf-green gabardine (E); sage-green corduroy (F); brown needlecord (G); dark-green towelling (H); sage-green gabardine (I); lime-green silk (J); cream bouclé (K).

Rug canvas – 25 × 50cm (9⅞ × 19⅝in).

Rug wools in light, mid- and dark browns, and greens.

Embroidery threads in a variety of green shades.

Tapestry wools in shades of green and chocolate brown.

Sewing threads to match oddment fabrics.

Fabric paint.

Oddments of wadding.

Oddments of knitting wools in mottled greens.

Rug hook.

Embroidery ring – 20cm (7⅞in) in diameter.

Making Up the Design

1 Following Fig 65, draw design on tracing paper. Trace off the sky area and cut out in wadding and grey poplin. Place the poplin over the wadding and position centrally on the hessian. For stitch instructions, see Chapter 3. Turn under the top and side edges of the poplin and slipstitch edges in place. Using fabric paints, paint in a storm-cloud effect on the poplin, using varying shades of white and grey. Work random single stitches through all layers to give depth and shape to sky.

2 Following tracing-paper drawing, trace off all hill areas and cut them out in the fabrics indicated. With work in embroidery ring, machine the pieces in position, using a wide, close satin stitch; start with the top section B and change the colour of thread to match the fabric being appliquéd. Make sure pieces are slightly overlapped so that none of the base fabric shows through.

3 Trace off foreground area onto rug canvas. The centre section is stitched while the foreground is hooked. For the stitched area use a half-cross stitch and mix the different-coloured tapestry threads and embroidery wools together to give a dense, mottled effect. Work the hooked area in the same mix of threads, using shades of both green and brown and trimming the tufts to give an irregular long-and-short rugged effect.

4 Cut out shapes of sheep from cream bouclé and hand-stitch in place on rugwork, padding them out with a little wadding. Using brown tapestry wool and blanket stitch, embroider legs and faces. Hand-sew rugwork to lower section of design.

5 Using knitting wools, knit circles of stitches about 6cm (2⅜in) in diameter for trees. Run a gathering thread round the outer edge of circles and stuff lightly. Sew these in position on the appliquéd section at either side, just above rugwork. Using brown tapestry wool and blanket stitch, work tree-trunks at base of knitted circles.

Fig 65 Diagram of Rain Clouds Over the Beacons

Manx Morning

This wall-hanging is constructed by needle-weaving wool yarns through a base of cotton warp threads. The design showing the southern point of the Isle of Man is woven using wool hand-spun from Manx fleeces; the subtle mix of colours is obtained from natural dyes. (Colour photograph opposite.)

Materials

Weaving-loom or frame at least 30cm (11¾in) wide and 40cm (15¾in) long.

Cream-cotton two-ply thread for warp thread and bottom and top borders.

Home-spun wools in various shades of green, brown, beige, cream, pink and mauve.

5mm (¼in) wide wooden dowelling – 32cm (12½in) long.

Light-coloured felt-tip pen.

Making Up the Design

1 Following the section on weaving in Chapter 3, set up a frame or loom with cotton warp thread covering an area no less than 30cm (11¾in) wide and at least 40cm (15¾in) long. Referring to Fig 66 (page 88), trace the design onto paper then lightly mark out these design lines on the warp threads using felt-tip pen.

2 Starting 5cm (2in) up from the base of the warp threads, work a 1cm (⅜in) band of weft threads, using the same cotton thread as for the warp threads. The weft thread can be taken behind and in front of either one or two threads at a time.

3 Continue needle-weaving design using wool yarns. Work over the same number of threads as for the beginning border, making sure that each row of weaving is packed down tightly to prevent warp threads from showing. If several colours of thread are to be used along one row of weaving, make sure the two thread-ends are secured tightly at the back of the weaving.

Use various shades of green and brown for the foreground hills with lighter shades towards the top of this area. Use cream for the base of the house and dark brown for its roof. The sea and sky area should be worked in shades of pink and mauve, intermixing them within one line of weaving and adding cream stitches worked to represent a cloud. The island in the middle of the design should be worked in a variety of brown and green shades.

4 When woollen work is complete, work 1cm (⅜in) of weaving in warp cotton thread again. Divide warp threads into groups about 3cm (1⅛in) wide and weave each of these groups separately for 2–3cm (¾–1⅛in) (this forms small lengths which will be turned into hanging loops).

5 Remove the weaving from the loom or frame. At the top edge, knot each pair of warp threads and cut off close to weaving. Make every other strap into a hanging loop, stitching the end down to the wrong side of the top of the weaving; roll remainder to the wrong side and stitch neatly out of view. Make a hole through each end of dowelling and thread a length of cotton thread through both holes to form a hanging thread.

6 At lower edge, knot warp threads together in groups of four and trim ends to form a straight fringe about 4cm (1½in) long.

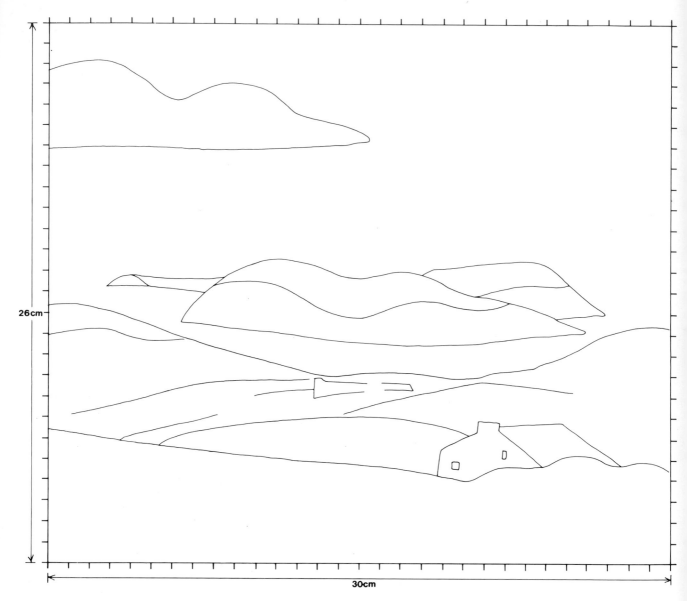

26cm

30cm

Fig 66 Diagram of Manx Morning

GILLIAN HICKMAN

Tranquillity

In this meeting of land, sea and sky, the coloured background fabric represents all three elements. The areas of spaced stitchery contrast with the densely stitched cliffs and delicately worked cottages. (Colour photograph page 90.)

Materials

Grey-green even-weave fabric – 35 × 40cm (13¾ × 15¾in).

Stranded cotton in shades of blue, shades of green, brown, turquoise, beige, grey and white, plus small amounts of black, terracotta, dark red, yellow and pink.

Fine tapestry wool in pale and mid-green and mid- and dark brown.

Embroidery ring – 30cm (11¾in) in diameter.

Making Up the Design

1 Following Fig 67 and referring to Transferring Your Design onto Fabric (Chapter 1), mark out the design on the centre of the fabric and insert in embroidery ring. For stitch instructions, see Chapter 3.

2 Work top of near cliff in mid-green tapestry wool using split stitch. Work the lines of stitching parallel to top edge of cliff and pack rows closely together.

3 Using two strands of dark-green stranded cotton, work small areas on top of middle cliff in satin stitch, main area of far cliff top in mid-green split stitch, and smaller part in mid-green satin stitch.

4 Stitch cliff faces, intermixing rows of pale-grey, beige and white stem stitch and split stitch. Vary rows, using one, two or three strands of stranded cotton. Use mainly fine threads on far cliffs and introduce thicker ones on the nearer cliffs.

Fig 67 Diagram of Tranquillity

18cm

26cm

5 Using stranded cotton (two strands), work curved shoreline in beige satin stitch; fill in foreground field with rows of densely packed stem stitch in shades of pale and mid-green.

6 Fill in beyond shoreline to the left and along the base of near cliffs with randomly spaced straight stitches in green, brown, grey and beige. Use a single strand of stranded cotton and allow background fabric to show through.

7 Using one or two strands of stranded cotton, add random French knots in greys and browns along inner shoreline, continuing across base of near cliff where they should be more densely packed. Stitch a few more French knots at base of far cliff.

8 Work trees and bushes at both sides of cove in stranded cotton; work trunks and branches in brown straight stitch (one strand), and leaves in French knots in varying shades of green (two strands).

9 Stem stitch lines on sky using two strands of pale-blue thread, and lines on sea in shades of turquoise, using one strand.

10 Using one strand of stranded cotton, work houses in beige, brown, red, grey and terra-cotta. Outline houses in straight or stem stitch. Fill in roofs in one of the following ways: with spaced single fly stitches, with spaced lines of couching or with closely worked satin stitch.

11 Add texture to house walls with spaced seed stitches. Satin stitch doors and windows in black or brown and fill in chimney-pots using satin stitch.

12 Add greenery to front of houses with spaced fly stitches and straight stitches. Work small trees and bushes as before (8). Using one strand, stitch flowers with green straight stitches and pink and yellow French knots.

13 Using tapestry wools in mid- and dark brown and pale and mid-green, stitch tree in foreground in same way as other trees. Stem stitch green lines on foreground in tapestry wools, and add a few spaced single fly stitches around the base of the tree.

14 Fill in the darker green area near base of tree in random straight stitches and French knots, using stranded cotton (two strands).

15 Stem stitch road in shades of beige and grey stranded cotton. Vary texture by intermixing rows of one, two and all six strands of thread.

16 Work fence-posts in split stitch using brown tapestry wool. Make fence links by threading a single strand of black thread under the posts and securing at the far and near ends.

17 Using shades of pale-green stranded cotton (two strands), straight stitch tufts of grass along bottom of fence, and stem stitch short random lines between the fence and the road.

CELIA FREAR

St Mary's Island

A seaside scene that on first appearance seems to be worked in simple appliqué. Look closer and you will see that there are interesting stitches worked in a variety of threads, with beads added, to give the textural effect of the coastline. (Colour photograph below.)

Materials
Pale green-grey furnishing tweed – 55 × 65cm (21⅝ × 25½in).
Oddments of white, grey, black, green, tan and chocolate felt.
Oddments of woollen fabric in buttermilk, and beige and tan mottled tweed.
Selection of sewing threads from embroidery silks to tapestry wools in grey, black, beige, white, a variety of greens, blues, yellow and silver.
Small beads in yellows, browns, white, clear, pearl, greens and blues.
Two small star sequins.
6mm (¼in) wide pale-blue ribbon – 30cm (11¾in).
Oddment of wadding.
Fabric adhesive.
Embroidery ring – 30cm (11¾in) in diameter.

Making Up the Design
1 Following Fig 68, draw the design on tracing paper. Trace off shapes in the following colours and cut out in felt: use white for the lighthouse and the two houses to the left of it (with black for the roof of the half-hidden house); tan for the roof of the near house; tan for the houses to the left of the lighthouse with chocolate for their roofs; green for the doors of the houses, grey for

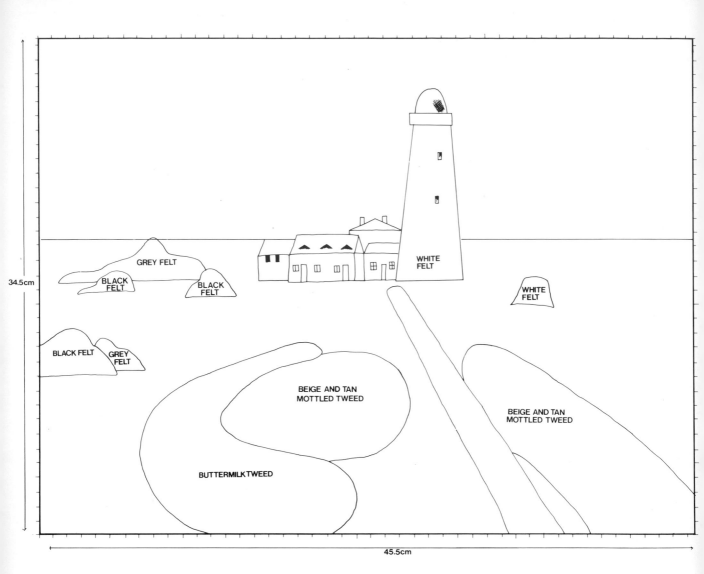

Labels visible in diagram: GREY FELT, BLACK FELT, BLACK FELT, WHITE FELT, WHITE FELT, BLACK FELT, GREY FELT, BEIGE AND TAN MOTTLED TWEED, BEIGE AND TAN MOTTLED TWEED, BUTTERMILK TWEED, 34.5cm, 45.5cm

Fig 68 Diagram of St Mary's Island

the pathway running down from the lighthouse and for the rocks to the left of the lighthouse; and black for the rocks to the left-hand corner of the design. Cut out the curved sand shape in buttermilk tweed; the two remaining large areas shown on the diagram should be cut out in the beige and tan mottled tweed.

2 Draw the basic outline of the design onto the base fabric, following Transferring Your Design onto Fabric (Chapter 1), and glue the felt pieces in place. Place the three tweed sections in position, put a little wadding under each piece and tack in place (this tacking should be removed when the design is complete).

3 Embroider detail on the lighthouse and houses (for stitch instructions, see Chapter 3): use black sewing thread and back stitch to outline the houses, doors, windows and chimneys; use white sewing thread in the same way to outline

windows of the tan-coloured house. Outline the brown roofs with couched tapestry wool.

4 Sew a length of ribbon along the horizon, either side of the lighthouse.

5 The remainder of the design is made up mainly of rows of various stitches · in a variety of different yarns and colours. Almost any stitches can be used – on this design they include blanket stitch, couching, satin, feather, straight and chain stitches. Beads are sewn on to highlight details and give texture, as are French knots. Knotted chain stitch in white yarn is used to depict the foam of the waves.

Start at the left-hand side and embroider grey satin stitch between the houses and grey-felt rocks. Fill in above this with rows of stitching in pale blue, silver and white, working a few rows above attached ribbon.

6 Using grey tapestry wool, work stitch detail in front of rocks and houses. Using a mixture of green threads together with greys and beige,

work grassy section in front of buildings and lighthouse. Work a few rows of white knotted stitch about 2.5cm (1in) down from attached ribbon on the right-hand side and fill in area above this to match left side.

7 Fill in area between two clumps of rocks on the left with rows of white and pale-blue embroidery, adding texture with clumps of French knots.

8 Now fill in the remainder of the foreground using beige, yellow and white threads either side of the work, adding the occasional stitch in black thread to give a contrast of colour. Fill in the centre area around the grey-felt path using shades of grey and blue thread and working slightly over tweed patches so they are securely caught down to the base fabric.

9 Finish the design with the addition of clumps of beads sewn on at various areas – clear beads in the water and other colours on the sand and rocks. Attach the two sequins as starfish to the tweedy area to the right of the foreground.

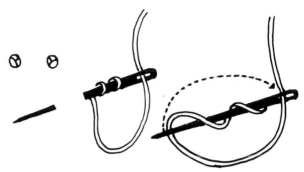

French knot

ISABEL BLINCOW

Yorkshire Farmhouse

This striking work uses the simplest techniques – appliqué and free-machine embroidery. The choice of fabrics reflects the varying textures and landscape depicted in this rural scene. (Colour photograph opposite.)

Materials

Cream backing fabric – 60 × 70cm (23⅝ × 27½in).

Cream net – 30 × 70cm (11¾ × 27½in).

Oddments of the following fabrics: dark-brown mottled cotton (A); green printed net (B); brown and cream patchy gabardine (C); cream and honey printed jersey (D); mottled brown-grey jersey (E); mink poplin (F); beige poplin (G); yellow even-weave rayon (H); orange and yellow printed rayon (J); sage-green lightly printed cotton (K).

Oddments of yellow, blue, beige, tan and brown net.

Sewing threads to match appliqué fabrics.

Embroidery ring – 20cm (7⅞in) in diameter.

Adhesive.

Making Up the Design

1 Following Fig 69 and referring to Transferring Your Design onto Fabric (Chapter 1), draw the design to full size on tracing paper. Use this to trace off the various pieces of appliqué and to get the right proportions for the design.

2 Cut out wispy cloud shapes in various sizes from the coloured nets (except cream) and stick to sky area of base fabric. Cover entire area with cream net, finishing along the horizon line.

3 The design is worked in sections of appliqué fabrics which are cut out in the material indicated then sewn down to the base fabric using machine satin stitch. The exception is the net area in the foreground. This section is held in place with jagged rows of random straight stitching following the print on the net; loosen the bobbin tension and use white thread on the bobbin so that small loops of white thread pull through to the right side to form a spotty effect.

4 Insert the work in the embroidery ring. Start the

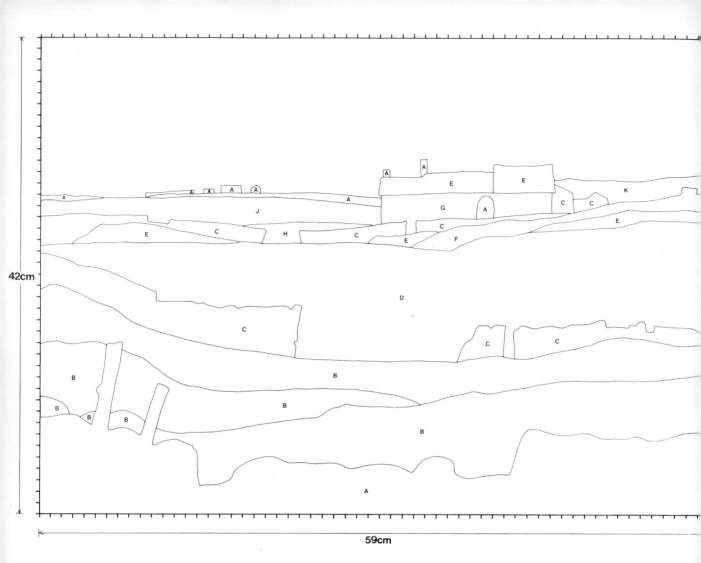

42cm

59cm

Fig 69 Diagram of Yorkshire Farmhouse

appliqué work with the fabrics appliquéd to the horizon. Next the field is depicted with an orange and yellow printed rayon fabric. Then the farmhouse is worked, with the windows worked in closely spaced satin stitch using dark-brown thread. Lines of straight stitching can be worked over the various areas in toning threads to give extra depth and added texture.

5 Appliqué the walls around the farmhcuse in the various brown fabrics indicated, changing the stitch width along the appliqué edge from time to time to give a rugged effect. Work the outline of the gate in machine satin stitch, using brown thread.

6 Appliqué the cream and honey jersey section in place, adding jagged lines of straight stitching towards the top edge of the piece.

7 Machine the walls to the right and left side of the design, working brick-like lines over these areas in dark-brown thread. Add fence and wire detail to the wall on the right, using a combination of machine straight stitching and satin stitch.

8 Appliqué the net section in position, following the directions given for stitching in (3).

9 Machine the foreground area of dark-brown mottled cotton in position, using a wide satin stitch. Work boulder-like lines over this in random dark-brown stitching.

10 Add a few machine-stitched bird images to the net sky area.

Summer Lake

This delicate and unusually textured picture is made from fine strips of fabric and yarn sewn into a gauzy background. (Colour photograph page 98.)

Materials

Loosely woven fabric (such as organdie) – 30 × 45cm (11¾ × 17¾in).

Oddments of all sorts of lightweight fabrics in shades of green, brown, grey and pale-blue lining, voile, chiffon, shirting and poplin (for greater individuality, why not try dyeing the fabrics to a selection of colours you'd like to use).

Tapestry wools and knitting yarns in shades of bright, light, dull green and grey.

Needle with a very large eye.

Making Up the Design

1 Following Fig 70 and referring to Transferring Your Design onto Fabric (Chapter 1), mark out the design on the centre of the fabric.
2 Cut fabrics into 5mm (¼in) wide strips, making sure they will fit through the needle eye. Use these strips as you would any thread, to fill in the blocks of colour. The design is worked entirely in small straight stitches 6–8mm (¼–⅜in) long, stitched in varying directions according to area to be filled (that is, tree-trunk is worked vertically whilst lake is worked horizontally).

Fig 70 Diagram of Summer Lake

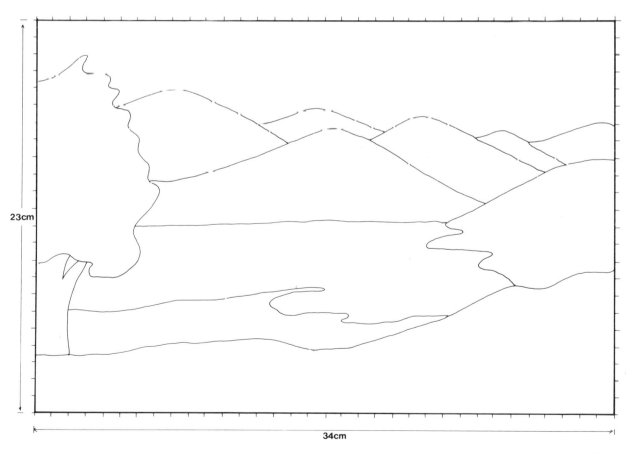

23cm

34cm

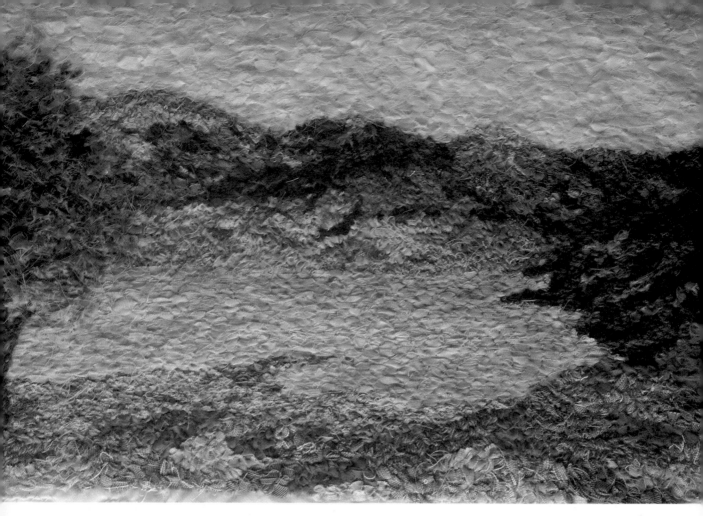

3 Fill in the sky area with very pale-blue strips. Work the lake in the same way, using deeper blue strips.

4 Work the foreground hills in shades of grey, intermixing the fabric strips with yarns; when using yarns, thread needle with three or four strands to give a thickness similar to that of fabric strips. The grassy section at base of central hill and to the right of the tree is worked in pale greens.

5 Work hills to the right-hand side of design in dark greens and browns, using yarns together with fabric strips. The remaining hills, with the exception of the brown peak on the central hill, are worked in mid-green using yarn and fabric strips.

6 Complete the tree-trunk and branches in shades of brown. The leaf section is worked entirely in fabric strips in shades of green with the stitches worked slightly more loosely than previously; leave a few short ends on right side to give a bushy look.

EILEEN SMITH

This Green and Pleasant Land

This knitted panel combines many different textures and types of yarns and shows how effective the simplest techniques can be. A little surface embroidery worked after the piece has been knitted adds extra depth of colour. (Colour photograph page 30.)

Materials

Oddments of the following yarns: mottled green 3-ply (A); brown DK (B); stone 3-ply (C); brown and beige slub chunky (D); emerald and cream slub chunky (E); orange, emerald and yellow bouclé (F); cyclamen bouclé (G); cream and beige slub DK (H); denim-blue bouclé (J); spearmint-green bouclé (K); turquoise 2-ply mohair (L); cream DK mohair (M); pale-blue 2-ply (N); lilac mohair (P); black and cream mohair (Q); pink and blue mixture mohair (R); sage and pale-green 3-ply (S and T); beige DK mohair (U); red and black fine mohair (V).
Oddments of a red, brown and green striped tweed.
Knitting needles, size 4mm (No 8).
Cable needle.

Making Up the Design

1 This design is worked almost entirely in stocking stitch (see Chapter 3) with a small amount of embroidery added after the knitting is completed. Following Fig 71, draw design to full size and use this as a guide to positioning colours.

2 This is a random type of knitting in which colours are mixed within each row. Always wind one yarn round the other when changing colours to prevent holes appearing in the work. With yarn A used double, cast on sufficient stitches for the width of the work plus a small border on both sides. Knit 3–4cm (1–1½in) in A to give a small border before the visible part of the design.

3 Start to introduce section on the left in B yarn: intermix the colours gradually by working both colours in the same row (for instance, work three stitches in A then two stitches in B). Fade through into a few rows in both yarn A and yarn C worked together.

4 Work a couple of rows using D yarn, then a couple of rows using E: slip a few stitches over a few rows (using the cable needle) to give an elongated tree-trunk effect. Now work bouclé sections with F and G.

5 Change to H yarn and work about four rows, working a few cables or fancy stitches each side to thicken texture. Start to bring in J and K bouclé sections, keeping H at right-hand side.

6 Change to M yarn and work stocking stitch for the first few rows of this yarn, working L to the right-hand side. Continue with M, bringing in a few stitches worked in N and P for highlights. Change gradually to Q on the right-hand side and P yarn at the left. Work a couple of rows in M yarn again, then finish with a band of R taken slightly further than the finished edge of diagram to give a border across the top.

7 Using S and T, chain stitch by hand tree tops just above left-hand side of J area. Work a few chain stitches in U yarn between tree tops and L section. For stitch instructions, see Chapter 3.

8 Cut fabric into 1.5cm (2in) wide strips and weave in and out of the knitting in lower sections A and B. Work a few French knots to resemble poppies over this section using V; just below these work long straight stitches over the knitted stitches using B, to represent stalks.

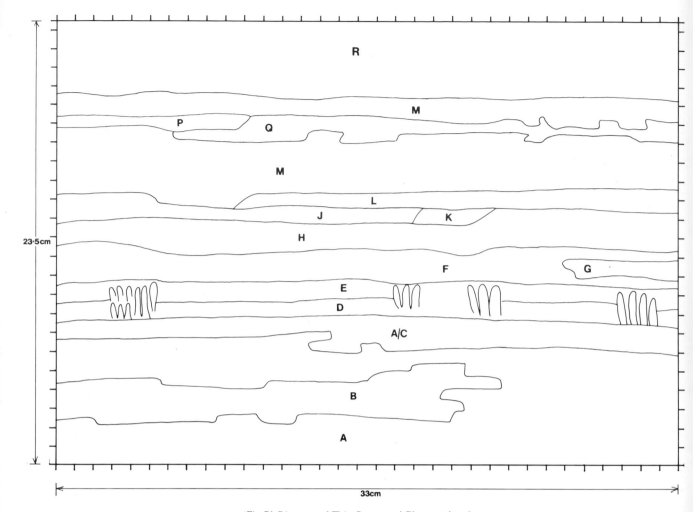

Fig 71 Diagram of This Green and Pleasant Land

KATE THORP

Summer Memories

The scene depicts a corner in a favourite public garden. Thick bouclé yarn, silky perlé cotton and the softest leather are used to create a rich and varied texture. (Colour photograph page 103.)

Materials

Dark-green hessian – 30 × 35cm (11¾ × 13¾in).
Dark-green lining fabric – 15cm (6in) square.
Pale-blue cotton fabric – 16 × 20cm (6¼ × 7⅞in).
Bouclé yarn in pale lime-green, plus small amounts of white and grey marl.
Perlé thread, No 5, in white, cream and pale lime-green.
Fine tapestry wool in light, mid- and dark green.
Coton à broder in pale and dark green and white.
Stranded cotton in soft and mid-greens.
Fine knitting yarn in a heathery mixture and soft mid-green (small amounts).
Small piece of soft, dark green leather.
Fabric adhesive.
Embroidery ring – 20cm (7⅞in) in diameter

Making Up the Design

1 Following Fig 72, draw design to full size on paper. Use hessian as background fabric, and draw the outside shape centrally onto the right-hand side. Tack pale-blue fabric for the sky to the hessian with its lower edge just overlapping the lowest part of sky area. Cut out lining fabric roughly to the shape of the large bobbly tree and tack to the background fabric at tree position. Lightly mark out other main areas of design on the fabric. Insert work in embroidery ring. For stitch instructions, see Chapter 3.

2 Work dark-green area of underlapping green leaves (lighter green bouclé leaves will later cover the majority of these stitches). Use green coton à broder, dark-green stranded cotton and a small amount of pale-green coton à broder, adding in dark-green tapestry wool at the left. Intermixing threads, stitch long straight stitches with some slightly at an angle to overlap others. Cover area densely, inter-

spersing these stitches with detached chain stitch.

3 Work the mid-green area below in the same way using tapestry wool, with a small area of soft-green stranded cotton (six strands) at the right near the tiny white flowers. Stitch over the tapestry wool with rows of open fishbone stitch worked downwards in green knitting yarn. Space stitches widely at the top and more closely at the bottom.

4 Stitch the lower right-hand corner in pale-green tapestry wool. Make straight stitches about 2cm (¾in) long, overlapping ends to fill the area. Stitch vertical stitches of uneven length across the rest of the lower edge in the grey marl bouclé yarn.

5 Fill in the area above the grey bouclé with long stitches in pale lime-green bouclé, overlapping ends of previous stitching at the top and bottom. Add long bullion stitches in the heathery yarn over the area of green stitches on the right, and at the top of bouclé stitches towards the left.

6 Using long straight stitches and white bouclé yarn, overstitch the area to left mid-picture. Satin stitch a small narrow band of pale-green tapestry wool above the dark-green area at left of design and a band of dark green above that.

7 Work the tree by first couching the lime-green bouclé yarn over the area: use a finer thread to couch the bouclé in place. Stitch more densely at the top and allow areas of the background to show lower down.

8 Work French knots over and among the bouclé using lime-green and white bouclé and white, cream and lime-green perlé thread. Intermix colours randomly, using the thicker thread towards the top.

9 Straight stitch star-like flowers over soft-green, stranded-thread stitches at right of design, using white perlé thread.

10 Cut out leaf shapes from soft green leather. Arrange underlapping shapes first and stick in place on right side of design, just above white flowers.

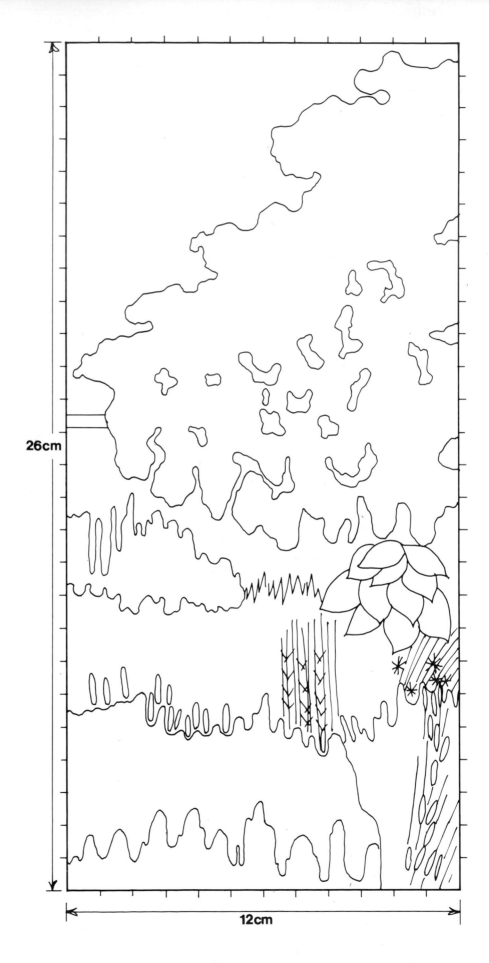

26cm

12cm

Fig 72 Diagram of
Summer Memories

The Old Mill

A small, intricate design, in which a simply painted background forms the base of the picture. The texture of the field is created with stitches in varying lengths of fine, stranded cotton, and the frail poppies are made of appliquéd organza. (Colour photograph page 6.)

Materials

Fine even-weave silk – 30cm (11¾in) square.
Stranded cotton in pale, medium and dark shades of soft green, plus small amounts of pale grey, dark grey, dark brown, camel and red.
Small piece of red organza.
Set of watercolours.
Embroidery ring – 20cm (7⅞in) in diameter.

Making Up the Design

1 Following Fig 73, draw design onto tracing paper. Position drawing in centre of fabric and lightly mark in horizon. Tape edges of fabric to a wooden board covered in paper.
2 Using blue watercolour, paint sky, shading from deep blue at the top to pale blue at horizon. When dry, paint pale green from horizon downwards, about 2cm (¾in) deep. Allow to dry.
3 Referring to Transferring Your Design onto Fabric (Chapter 1), lightly mark out the remaining features of the embroidery. Place work in embroidery ring. Divide thread and using two strands together, begin filling in the foreground. For stitch instructions, see Chapter 3. Working from horizon downwards, use pale green along horizon, then shade into medium green. Work in vertical straight stitches varying from about 5mm (¼in) long at horizon to 5cm (2in) long over foreground. Continue stitching until area is densely covered.
4 Using a single strand of dark brown, outline mill and houses at left of picture in long straight stitches. Satin stitch roofs and windows.
5 Using a single strand of camel thread, satin stitch roofs at the right of the picture.
6 Fill in around the mill and across the horizon with French knots, using a single strand of grey thread.
7 Return to the foreground to work texture detail over the long stitches with random spaced stitches. Work two or three fly stitches then fasten down with a long stitch. Also work some spaced fly stitches in the same way but use two strands of thread and mix medium- and dark-green shades.
8 Stitch long grasses in right foreground using single strands of thread and all shades of green. Stitch long straight stitches and some single fly stitches on long stalks. Work grass-heads by making bullion stitches of varying lengths.
9 Work stems for poppies in spaced fly stitch. Cut organza into 1.5–2cm (½–¾in) diameter circles. For closed poppies, fold circles into four. Tuck under point, and stitch onto work with fanned-out blanket stitch, using a single strand of dark green thread.
10 For open poppies, make a single tuck in the circle and stitch onto the work with tiny, dark-grey French knots, using a single strand of thread. Stitch poppy buds in detached chain stitches, using two strands of red.
11 Add more texture to right foreground with long bullion stitches, using two or three strands of mixed green threads. Also work random lengths of chain stitch using four strands of thread.

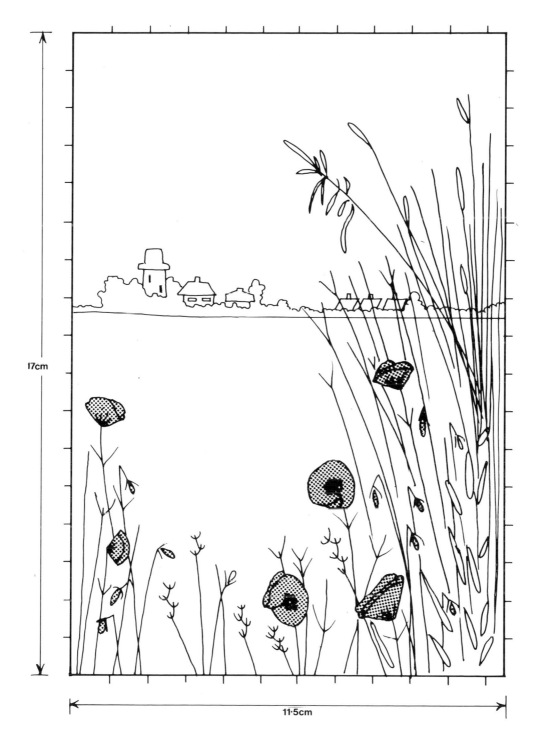

17cm

11·5cm

Fig 73 Diagram of The Old Mill

JOY BROWN

Summertime Reflections

This view of Old Scotney Castle combines appliqué, hand and machine embroidery. The reflection is given its misty hazy look by overlaying a piece of black net on the finished embroidery work. (Colour photograph opposite.)

Materials

Deep-blue hessian – 40 × 50cm (15¾ × 19⅝in).
Black net – 20 × 40cm (7⅞ × 15¾in).
Grey interfacing, lightweight iron-on – 60 × 70cm (23⅝ × 27½in).
Oddments of the following fabrics: rust corduroy (A); beige hessian (B); black and beige window-pane printed fabric (C); rust canvas (D); pale-green shantung (E); sage-green velvet (F); sage-green canvas (G); light green candlewick (H); brown mottled tweed (I); pale-green sateen (J).
Machine sewing thread to match appliqué fabric oddments.
Embroidery silks and tapestry wools in bright and dull greens, rust and dark browns, beige and grey, pink, lilac, primrose yellow and black.
Black felt-tip pen.
Embroidery ring – 20cm (7⅞in) diameter.

Making Up the Design

1 Following Fig 74, draw the design on tracing paper. Apply interfacing to the wrong side of the appliqué oddments, then cut out the various pieces in the fabrics indicated on the diagram. Apply interfacing to wrong side of hessian. For stitch instructions, see Chapter 3.
2 Each piece of the appliqué is first neatened separately with machine satin stitch on each edge, then machined to the work with straight stitch worked close to the satin-stitch edges. Using a medium-width closely worked machine zigzag stitch, neaten the edges of each piece of appliqué in a complementing colour thread. Insert work in ring.
3 Starting with the top hill to the left of the design, machine the green shantung piece in place, then the sage-green velvet and canvas pieces followed by the strip of candlewick.
4 Tack the pale-green sateen in place in front of castle. Machine the base of the house to the right of castle tower in place, making sure it overlaps top edge of green sateen. Machine roof and chimney sections in place, accentuating the base of the chimney with a row of closely worked machine zigzag stitch (machine satin stitch). Satin stitch chimney tops in rust sewing thread. Satin stitch windows to base and roof sections of house, together with the door and the small projecting roof on the corduroy roof section, which should slightly overlap window fabric.
5 Set machine to a very small straight stitch, then work lines of stitching to resemble bricks over remaining beige hessian oddment. With this completed, cut out castle tower and wall sections indicated on diagram. Machine the main section of the tower in place, then the corduroy roof, just overlapping the top edge of the hessian. Machine the satin-stitched window just off-centre on the tower. Machine smaller section of building to the right of the tower in place, then its roof and window.
6 Using tapestry wool in both dull and bright greens, work French knots around the stonework of the tower and house, mixing the colours together for a varied foliage.
7 Using dull-green tapestry wool, work a narrow band of stem stitch along front edge of house. Work a band of dark brown stem stitch below this, continuing the line along the entire lower edge of the tower and wall.
8 Work a narrow band of stem stitch at the top of the sage-green canvas section appliquéd on the left-hand side. Then above and below this line, work clumps of French knots in pink, lilac and primrose yellow, interspersed with the occasional green knot.
9 Begin to work the reflection of the castle and hill below the sage-green sateen. Working in stem stitch of various lengths, mirror the appliquéd image, although not in so much detail. Use a variety of tapestry wools and silks, keeping the image in darker tones than the appliquéd area.
10 Lay net over entire reflection and water area, cutting it to follow the contour of the sateen edge and hand stitching it down in this position. Lay another piece of net over the lower section of water at the base of the work,

Fig 74 Diagram of Summertime Reflections

stopping it about a third of the way up and securing it down with hand stitching.

11 Using stem stitch and bright-green tapestry wool, work clumps of leaves on the top of the net area. Highlight these clumps with lilies worked in splayed-out groups of chain stitch in shades of pink embroidery silk.

12 Using both embroidery and tapestry yarns, work reeds in lower left-hand corner of work using graduated lengths of stem stitch. Large lily leaves in lower right-hand corner are worked in hand satin stitch, using dull-green tapestry wool.

13 Using the felt-tip pen, draw arch-like curves across the tower and just above the satin-stitched window.

River Wey Backwater

Depicting a peaceful river bank, this design combines various types of threads and stitches with appliqué. The reflection is created by half the work being covered with organza, which gives this section a hazy feel. (Colour photograph pages 110–11.)

Materials

Pale-blue base fabric – 50cm (19⅝in) square.
Bright-green silk fabric – 40cm (15¾in) square.
Oddments of wadding and pale-blue chiffon.
Cream organza – 20 × 40cm (7⅞ × 15¾in).
Stranded cotton in dark, mid- and light greens, pink, cream, orange and marigold.
Embroidery silks in cream, a selection of greens, pink, cerise and marigold.
Tapestry wools in various shades of green, brown, beige and khaki.
Bright-green mohair yarn.
Fabric adhesive.
Metallic thread in pale and bright green, blue and pearlised.
Embroidery frame – 40cm (15¾in) square.

Making Up the Design

1 Following Fig 75 and referring to Transferring Your Design onto Fabric (Chapter 1), mark out the design on the centre of the fabric. To obtain the reflective feel of the design, the top half of the work should be completed and the reflection of that work carried out over the lower section. For stitch instructions, see Chapter 3.

2 Lightly glue wadding to sky and sky-reflection areas and leave to dry. When dry, pull off most of wadding to leave a wispy cloud effect. Cover upper sky section with pale-blue chiffon, taking it just over foliage area, and stitch in place. Lightly glue wadding over top half of foliage area. Cut out entire foliage section (including the reflection) in bright-green fabric and sew in position on work. Place work in embroidery frame.

3 Begin by embroidering the foliage area at the top of the design (the dotted line on the diagram indicates where the reflection starts). Emphasise the top edge of the foliage with tapestry wool and mohair yarn couched in position.

4 Work the tree-trunks with several rows of chain stitch using a variety of brown wools and silks. Give the appearance of branches to the trunk on the far right by couching a dark-green silk thread in a random shape.

5 Just above the dotted line on the left-hand side of the work, couch lines of green tapestry wool to give the appearance of a distant river bank. Repeat this couching above the dotted line on the right-hand side, using paler shades of tapestry wool and securing the threads down in a more random way than before. Work clumps of French knots over this area using stranded cotton (three threads) and embroidery silks in pinks, cerise and marigold. Work a mass of cream embroidery-silk knots towards the left edge of this bank. Add the odd detached chain stitch among the French knots, using brown tapestry wool.

6 Work French knots over the remaining foliage area. Use a variety of threads in various shades of green, working the knots more densely in some areas than others.

7 Having completed the top half of the work, begin embroidering the reflection. The work should be a mirror-image of the top half, although it should appear a little more hazy and therefore the work can be a little less detailed.

8 Place the organza over the reflection embroidery, and stitch in place along the two river banks. Sew a few rows of couched green

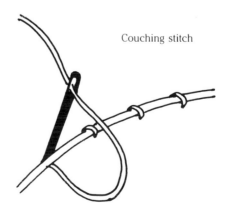

Couching stitch

River Wey Backwater,
see page 109

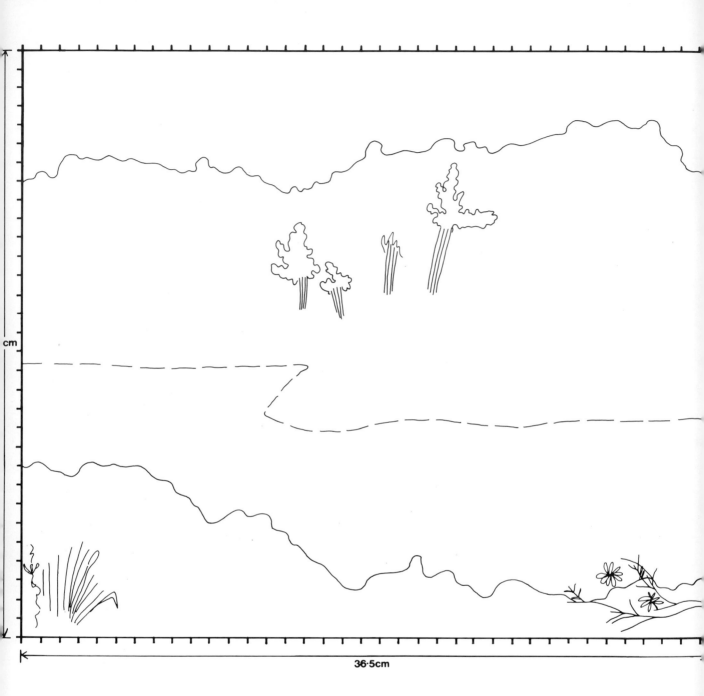

cm

36·5cm

Fig 75 Diagram of River Wey Backwater

tapestry thread along the bank in the foreground, over the edge of the organza and emphasise with a few detached chain stitches worked in six strands of green cotton.

9 Work flowers and leaves at the bottom right-hand corner. Using green stranded cotton (three threads) and detached chain stitch, work leaf shapes over this area. Give the appearance of stalks by working rows of slipstitch in green threads between the leaves. Highlight this area with pale-pink detached chain stitch in small clusters.

10 Work the greenery at the bottom left-hand corner of the design using long straight stitches in a variety of different threads, all in various shades of green.

11 Complete the reflection with long and short straight stitches worked over the organza. Use the colour of metallic thread to match the area being worked over and keep all the stitches parallel with the river banks.

JANET PARKER

Winter Morning

The village scene is stitched boldly in silky threads which imitate the lustre of a frosty morning. The buildings are stitched in cable stitch, which contrasts with the chain-stitch swirls of green foliage. (Colour photograph page 115.)

Materials

Even-weave linen – 43 × 45cm (17 × 17¾in).

Stranded cotton in shades of lilac, violet, pale, mid- and bright pinks, pale and mid-blues, royal blue, pale, bright and dark greens, dull green, pale grey, brown, light and mid-beige and camel.

Shaded stranded cotton in pale blue and dark pink.

Perlé cotton, No. 5, in white, pale blue, pale pink and lemon.

Embroidery frame – 45cm (17¾in) square.

Making Up the Design

1 Following Fig 76 and referring to Transferring Your Design onto Fabric (Chapter 1), mark out the design centrally on the fabric. Attach fabric to embroidery frame. Use all six strands of stranded cotton except where perlé cotton is specified, in which case use two strands of perlé together. For stitch instructions, see Chapter 3.

2 Stem stitch bare tree and branches in stranded cotton. Work trees to left in alternate rows of brown and camel. Stitch centre tree in same way with one row of dull green at the right of the tree. Stitch distant trees at left in mid-beige and dull green, and distant trees at right in light beige and dull green.

3 Stem stitch trunk and branches of tall ever-green tree in brown. Chain stitch around the outline of green areas, then continue around the shape, filling in towards centre. Add lines of white perlé chain stitch to represent snow on the top of branches.

4 Stem stitch the bright-green tree below the tall tree. Work stitching upwards and outwards into the points of the branches. Add rows of white perlé stem stitch for snow along tops of branches.

5 House on the left: outline gable ends with white perlé chain stitch. Outline blue windows in white perlé back stitch. Back stitch royal-blue lines and fill in windows and downpipe in royal-blue satin stitch. Cable stitch lemon areas in perlé thread. Cable stitch roof using perlé for the white parts and shaded-blue stranded cotton for the rest. Cable stitch top of lower windows in pale-blue shades and strip below main roof in royal blue. Satin stitch chimney in bright pink and white perlé thread. Cable stitch smoke in lilac with pale grey at the centre.

6 Second house from left: outline gable with two rows of white perlé stem stitch. Below that, stitch white perlé running stitch interlaced with violet. Outline window in bright pink cable and fill in with vertical cable in violet and lemon perlé. Outline blue window in mid-blue chain stitch with a white perlé chain-stitch ledge, and fill in with violet cable stitch. Work vertical mid-blue cable stitch on pointed part of window.

7 Cable stitch chimney in bright and pale pink with a row of white perlé chain stitch for snow. Complete as for first house, using pink for walls. Add bright pink straight stitches down right-hand edge of wall.

8 Work houses to right in same way, using white perlé chain stitch to outline the gables. Work the bright-pink chimney on the right in vertical cable. Work other two chimneys in pale and bright-pink satin stitch with white perlé for snow. Stitch smoke in lilac.

9 Work church tower using beige vertical cable stitch for the corners and horizontal cable stitch across the front. Add in a few brown straight stitches among the beige. Outline front windows in brown stem stitch and fill in all windows in violet vertical cable stitch. Add two pale-blue straight stitches at top of front windows and white perlé satin stitch on ledges for snow.

10 Stem stitch main struts of spire with a row of light beige and a row of violet, using a single strand only. Fill in spire with stem stitch in pale blue and white perlé. Stitch weathercock and square above side window in lemon perlé.

11 Work garage roof in same way as previous roofs. Cable stitch door and strip below roof in violet, and side wall in dark-pink stranded cotton. Using bright pink, cable stitch gable end and satin stitch either side of doorway.

33cm

35cm

Fig 76 Diagram of Winter Morning

Cable stitch a line in bright pink around the door and down corner of wall. Outline front edge of gable in pale-blue stem stitch, then outline gable with two rows of white perlé chain stitch interlaced with violet thread.

12 Stem stitch vertical lines on wall in dark-pink shaded thread. Stitch wall in dark-pink shaded cable stitch with a band of white perlé cable stitch at the top.

13 Stitch branches behind wall in brown stem stitch. Using different shades of soft green, stitch bushes behind wall: stitch bushes on the right in cable stitch and the others behind the wall and garage in chain stitch, allowing stitches to follow the contour of the bushes. Stem stitch white perlé snow on top of bushes.

14 Working upwards, stitch the pale-green areas in cable stitch. Then cable stitch the pale-pink areas in pale-pink perlé and the slightly darker area in stranded cotton. Cable stitch the cloud in lilac. Starting from the top, cable stitch the sky in pale-blue perlé. Stitch birds in royal-blue straight stitch.

15 Return to foreground and stitch gate and fence in dark-brown cable stitch worked vertically, horizontally and diagonally. Stitch right-hand

side of uprights in beige and add a row of white perlé cable along the top of fence and gate, and satin stitch on top of posts.

16 Following the angle of the slope, cable stitch the foreground in white perlé, pale green and mid-blue. Outline straight edge of road in grey stem stitch, using two strands only. Cable stitch road with lilac at the centre, then grey, and white perlé at either side. Cable stitch area to left of road in white perlé.

17 Chain stitch branches of hedge to left of road in brown. Cable stitch around branches in dull green. Cable stitch white perlé snow along top of hedge and on branches. Fill in between branches with violet straight stitches and pale-blue straight stitches at the base. Add bright-green stem-stitched grasses at base of hedge and bright-pink French knots on hedge.

18 Chain stitch bushes behind the fence and hedge in soft greens with white perlé on top edges. Cable stitch the bright green hedge, adding a few white perlé straight stitches along the top. Chain stitch the bushes behind the hedge in brown, camel and white cotton.

19 Fill in remaining area of foreground around the gate in pale-blue shaded cable stitch, adding in a little soft green behind the gate. Stem stitch grasses either side of gateway in beige.

ISABEL BLINCOW

Welsh Bay

This seaside view combines the clever use of printed and textured fabric appliquéd using the free-machine embroidery technique – not a single stitch has been worked by hand. To achieve the subtlety of colour that this design requires, spend some time collecting the fabrics you would like to use for your design. (Colour photograph page 2.)

Materials

White-satin base fabric – 60 × 70cm (23⅝ × 27½in).

White net – 30 × 60cm (11¾ × 23⅝in) plus oddments of net in pale blue, pale yellow, pink, black and green.

Oddments of the following fabrics: khaki and turquoise mottled fabric (A); coarse-weave mottled blue fabric (B); speckled sandy fabric (C); khaki and cream bush-print fabric (D); blue-green grass-print fabric (E); sandy, green-grey bush-print fabric (F); beige ottoman (G); blue-grey mottled fabric (H); darker blue-grey mottled fabric (I); silver-grey satin (J); light-turquoise shantung (K); pale blue-green shantung (L).

Selection of sewing threads to match appliqué fabrics, plus white and a variety of tones of green, blue, cream and brown.

Silver lurex sewing thread.

Fabric adhesive.

Embroidery ring – 20cm (7⅞in) in diameter.

Making Up the Design

1 Following Fig 77, draw the design on tracing paper, and mark out the design lightly on the base fabric, referring to Transferring Your Design onto Fabric (Chapter 1).

2 Cover the sky area with white net, allowing it to go a little over the hill and horizon areas. Tack in place around all edges.

3 Following the diagram, cut out the shapes to be appliquéd in the fabrics indicated. Where one section of the design meets another, leave a small allowance on this edge so that the pieces can be placed over each other without any of the base fabric showing. The main sections of the design are appliquéd to the base fabric using a medium-width machine satin stitch and a thread colour similar to the fabric being appliquéd. The bush areas are appliquéd using a pre-set machine stitch to hold the pieces in place.

4 Place the work in embroidery ring. Begin with the sea sections which stretch along the horizon and in front of the hills. Using the silver lurex thread on the top of the machine and a grey thread on the bobbin, machine the sections in place.

5 Appliqué the hills in position. Alter the machine to a straight stitch and using the same thread colour, work lines of stitching over the hills, following the outer contours (a small area of the hill indicated on the diagram has an overlay of black net laid on before the stitching is completed – this gives the hill depth and texture).

6 Appliqué the sand section in place, giving the top edge of the sand a band of white satin stitch.

7 Appliqué the main building sections in place with thread of a similar colour, then with a slightly lighter thread define the corners and chimneys of the buildings. The top of the door and windows are highlighted with pale-blue satin stitch and the windows with vertical rows of black satin stitch.

8 Appliqué the roofs in position. To give the roofs depth, change the machine to a straight stitch and using the same colour of thread as for the roof, work lines of stitching over the roofs, parallel to roof edges. Still using straight stitch but changing to mid-blue thread, work brick-like lines over the fronts of the two central buildings.

9 Place small pieces of black net over the buildings at the green bush areas, then, working with various shades of green thread, embroider over the net using a random zigzag stitch (set the machine to a zigzag stitch and as you work, move the embroidery ring under the needle).

10 Appliqué the stone walls in position, using a grey satin stitch along the bottom edge and

Fig 77 Diagram of Welsh Bay

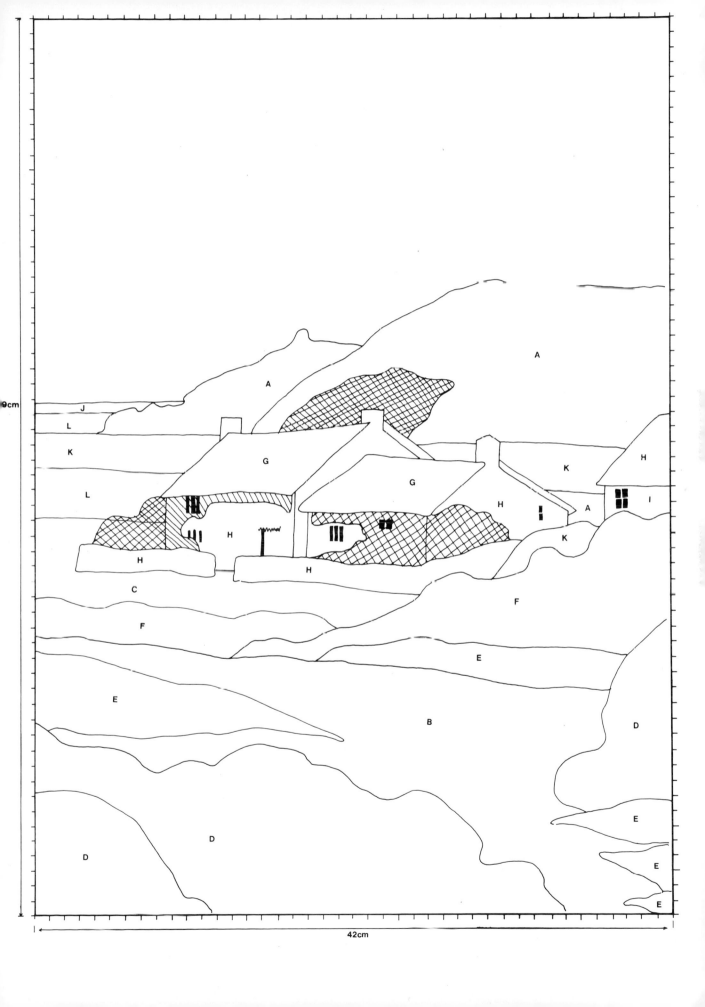

white along the top. Change to a straight stitch and blue thread and work stone-like lines over the wall sections.

11 Place the darker blue-grey mottled fabric in place with the sandy green-grey bush-print sections overlapping the top edge of this. Secure the bushes in place using a pre-set machine stitch and a variety of cream and brown threads (loosening the bobbin thread tension will help to give the machine stitch an added surface texture).

12 Place the blue-green grass-print sections on the work and secure to the base fabric in the same way, using pale-blue and green threads. Repeat this method with the bushes set to the forefront of the design, changing the colour thread to suit the section of fabric being appliquéd.

13 Work some extra sections of stitching to give the design added depth of colour. Using a sand-coloured thread, work random-length lines of straight stitch in front of the stone walls; changing to a dark-grey thread, work similar lines of stitching over the darker, blue-grey mottled fabric, progressing from the middle of this section out towards the bushes.

14 Take the work out of the ring. Cut out cloud shapes in the various colours of net; remove the tacking and, holding the white net in place, arrange the clouds under the white net. When you are satisfied with their position, fix them in place with small dots of adhesive.

15 Set the machine to satin stitch and using white thread, embroider a few bird-like shapes over the sky and hill areas. Work more distant bird shapes on the sky using a brown-coloured thread.

Stockists

Dryad, PO Box 38, Northgates, Leicester LE1 9BU
Supplier of a wide variety of craft items. The comprehensive catalogue includes everything from felt and canvas to spray paints and frames.

Dylon International Ltd, London SE26 5HD
Suppliers of a wide range of chemical dyes including fabric paints 'Color Fun' now widely used in conjunction with embroidery techniques.

Ells & Farrier, 5 Princes Street, London W1
An extensive range of beads plus unusual cords and chains sold by the metre.

English Sewing Ltd, PO Box 245, 56 Oxford Street, Manchester M60 1HJ
They will provide useful information on machine embroidery plus the right threads to choose.

John Lewis, Oxford Street, London W1
Apart from stocking a wide range of dressmaking and furnishing fabrics they stock embroidery articles and are happy to provide a mail order service.

Liberty and Co, Regent Street, London W1
Known for their beautiful range of fabrics they stock some of the more unusual threads for embroidery plus a good supply of DMC threads.

Royal School of Needlework, 25 Princes Gate, London SW7 1QE
Apart from running courses and lectures, this establishment houses a comprehensive shop stocking most embroidery articles. They also provide a service for mounting completed work.

The British Needlecrafts Council, The Old Vicarage, Hayley Hill, Halifax HX3 6DR.
A trade association and sponsors of the Needlecrafts Club. They are happy to supply information on manufacturers of needlecraft products.

The Embroiderers Guild, Apartment 41A Hampton Court Palace, East Molesey, Surrey KT8 9AU

The Quilters Guild, Clarendon, 56 Wilcot Road, Pewsey, Wiltshire SN9 5EL

Bibliography

Here is a list of books that I have found particularly inspiring and I'm sure anyone interested in fresh ideas will too.

Dalby, Gill *Spinning and Dyeing* (David & Charles, 1984)
A really good book on spinning and dyeing, well illustrated, with simple instructions for a wealth of natural dyes.

Fassett, Kaffe *Glorious Knitting* (Century Publishing, 1985)
A wonderful book on knitting with inspirational ideas that translate well into embroidery as well as knitting. The colours and patterns included are very beautiful.

Foster, Julia *Julia Foster's Patchwork* (Elm Tree Books/Hamish Hamilton Ltd, 1985)
If you would like to try various types of patchwork, this book written in the most appealing way will get you started.

Good Housekeeping *Patchwork and Appliqué* (Dorling Kindersley, 1981)
A small pocket-sized book giving concise instructions together with inspiring ideas beautifully photographed.

Good Housekeeping *Quilting and Patchwork* (Dorling Kindersley, 1983)
In the same series as the previous book, this small but comprehensive book includes some beautiful needlework examples.

Jackson, Valerie *The Complete Book of Patchwork and Quilting* (Century Publishing, 1981)
Everything you need to know about the subject plus exciting design ideas.

Thompson, Flora *The illustrated Lark Rise to Candleford* (Century Publishing, 1984)
The prettiest of books to inspire you with countryside scenes. The colour prints are particularly lovely.

Index